THOMAS GAINSBOROUGH

The Harvest Wagon

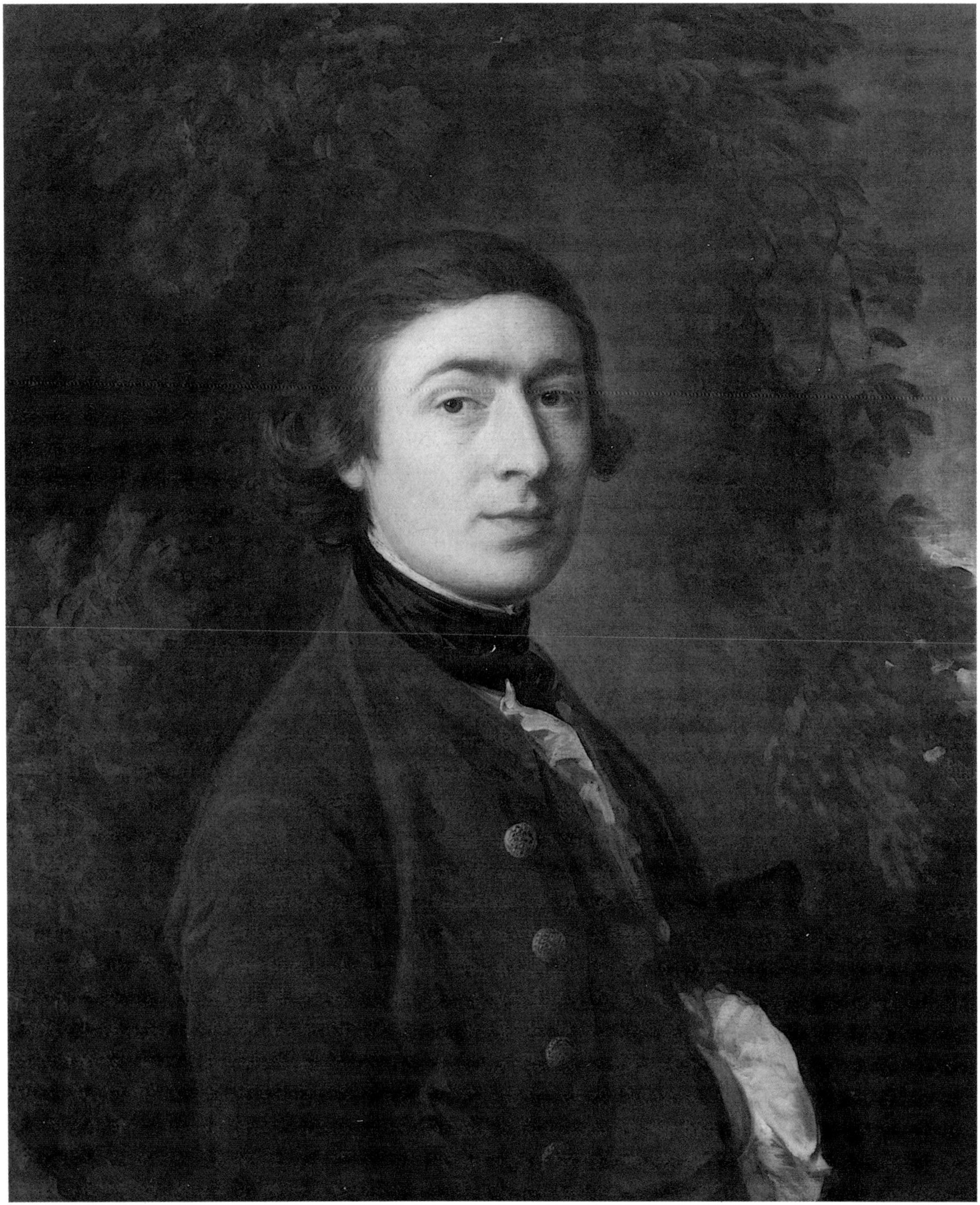

Thomas Gainsborough: *The Artist in his Early Thirties* (cat. 4).

THOMAS GAINSBOROUGH

The Harvest Wagon

Paul Spencer-Longhurst
and
Janet M. Brooke

Birmingham Museum and Art Gallery
28 April – 9 July 1995
Art Gallery of Ontario, Toronto
29 July – 9 October 1995

An exhibition mounted in collaboration with
The Barber Institute of Fine Arts,
The University of Birmingham

Front cover:
Details of *The Harvest Wagon*, 1767, The Barber Institute of Fine Arts
The Harvest Wagon, 1784/5, Art Gallery of Ontario.

Published and © Copyright 1995 by
Birmingham Museums and Art Gallery, The Trustees of the Barber Institute of Fine Arts
The University of Birmingham and Art Gallery of Ontario, Toronto

The Art Gallery of Ontario is funded by the Ontario Ministry of Culture, Tourism and Recreation. Additional operating support is received from the Municipality of Metropolitan Toronto, the Department of Canadian Heritage and The Canada Council.

ISBN 0704415232
Paul Spencer-Longhurst and Janet M. Brooke

Project management by Magnolia Concept, Stratford upon Avon
Designed by Krome, Cambridgeshire
Set in Palatino by Goodfellow & Egan Phototypesetting Ltd, Cambridgeshire
Printed in England by Printstream Ltd, Leicestershire

Contents

Preface

Thomas Gainsborough: 'The Harvest Wagon' is the third in the series of exhibitions held jointly by Birmingham Museum and Art Gallery and the Barber Institute of Fine Arts, and designed to highlight the quality and importance of collections in the city of Birmingham. It breaks significant new ground, however, with the full involvement of a major trans-Atlantic sister institution, the Art Gallery of Ontario. For the first time residents of Birmingham and Toronto will have the opportunity to see together in their own cities two of the most spectacular landscapes painted by one of England's greatest landscapists. It is particularly appropriate that the exhibition should open in Birmingham since, not only has the earlier version of *The Harvest Wagon* been housed in the Barber Institute at the University of Birmingham for almost half a century, but the later version also belonged in the mid-nineteenth century to a Birmingham collector, John Gibbons.

The exhibition has been organised jointly by Paul Spencer-Longhurst, Curator of the Barber Institute, and Janet M. Brooke, Independent Curator, Art Gallery of Ontario. Together they have devised a carefully focused selection of works by means of which to explore the recurring theme of the harvest wagon in Gainsborough's art, and to demonstrate the breadth and evolution of his landscape style from his early to his late career.

As always with a small, precise exhibition we have been dependent upon the close co-operation of certain key lenders, for whose generosity we are sincerely grateful. Several of the works on show normally grace the walls of private collectors, and to them we particularly acknowledge our debt for their willingness to be deprived of their treasures over a period of six months. We are also most grateful to the British Museum for lending no fewer than nine prints and drawings.

The Trustees and staffs of the Barber Institute and the Art Gallery of Ontario have provided support for this project from its inception over four years ago. In addition to the exhibition's co-curators and their colleagues at both institutions, we also acknowledge the substantial contribution of our colleagues at Birmingham Museum and Art Gallery towards the realisation of this exhibition, in particular, Richard Lockett, who has essentially made the whole project work, Stephen Wildman, Elizabeth Smallwood, Peter Butler and Haydn Roberts.

Thomas Gainsborough: 'The Harvest Wagon' enjoys the valued support of Shakespeares Solicitors, Birmingham and the British Council in Canada. The printing of the catalogue has been facilitated by a major grant from the Paul Mellon Centre for Studies in British Art. The Canadian presentation of the exhibition is sponsored by Goldman Sachs Canada. To all of these generous supporters we are most grateful.

Michael Diamond,
Assistant Director (Museums and Arts),
Birmingham Museums and Art Gallery

Glenn D. Lowry,
Director,
Art Gallery of Ontario

Richard Verdi,
Director, Barber Institute of Fine Arts,
University of Birmingham

Acknowledgments

Among the numerous contributors to the preparation of this exhibition and catalogue the authors would like to acknowledge with particular appreciation the co-operation, assistance and enthusiasm of Dr Brian Allen, Director of Studies, The Paul Mellon Centre for Studies in British Art, London; Hugh Belsey, Curator, Gainsborough's House, Sudbury, Suffolk; David A. Brenneman, Assistant Curator of Paintings, Yale Center for British Art: Sue Fryer; John Harniman and Sarah Dawbarn, The British Council in Canada; Dr John Hayes; Jan Johnson, Curator, Montreal Museum of Fine Arts; Martha Kelleher, Assistant Curator of European Art, Art Gallery of Ontario; Clare Lloyd-Jacob, The Paul Mellon Centre for Studies in British Art; Richard Lockett; Paul Mitchell, London; Jacquie Oliver; Karen Parker; Jane Sedge, Senior Assistant Curator, Christchurch Mansion, Ipswich; Dr Kim Sloan, Department of Prints and Drawings, British Museum; Susan Sloman, Curator, Victoria Art Gallery, Bath; Christine Smith; Nicholas Turner, Professor Richard Verdi, and Sophie Wilson.

Abbreviations

The following abbreviations have been used to refer to literature frequently cited in the text:

Fulcher: George Williams Fulcher, *Life of Thomas Gainsborough, R. A.*, London, 1856.

Hayes: John Hayes, *The Landscape Paintings of Thomas Gainsborough: A Critical Text and Catalogue Raisonné*, 2 vols, London and Ithaca (NY), 1982.

Hayes, *Drawings:* John Hayes, *The Drawings of Thomas Gainsborough*, 2 vols, London and New Haven, 1970.

Waterhouse: Ellis Waterhouse, *Gainsborough*, London, 1958.

Whitley: William T. Whitley, *Thomas Gainsborough*, London, 1915.

Woodall, *Letters:* Mary Woodall, ed., *The Letters of Thomas Gainsborough*, 2nd edition, London, 1963.

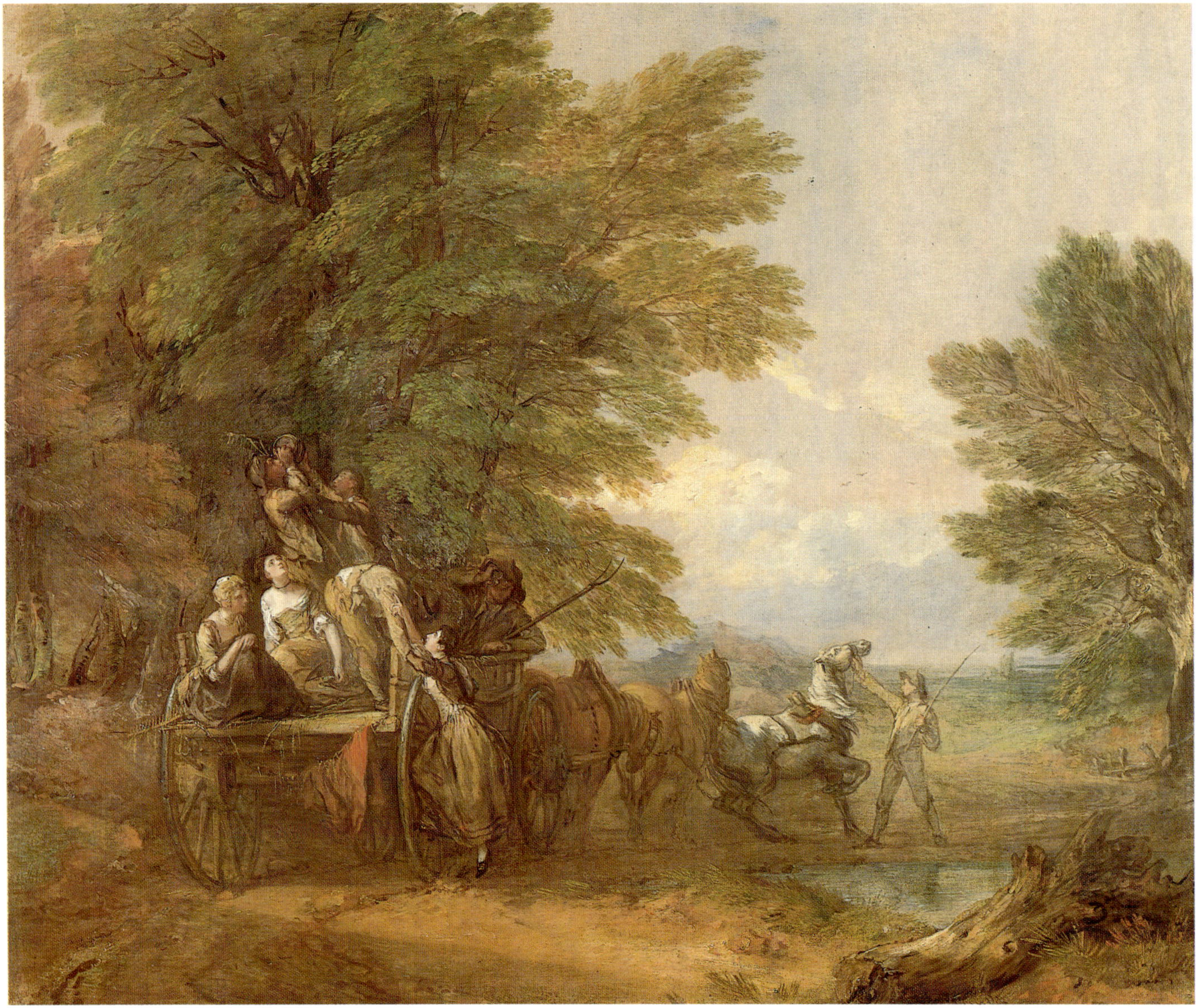

Plate I (cat. 1). Gainsborough, *The Harvest Wagon*, 1767
The Barber Institute of Fine Arts, The University of Birmingham

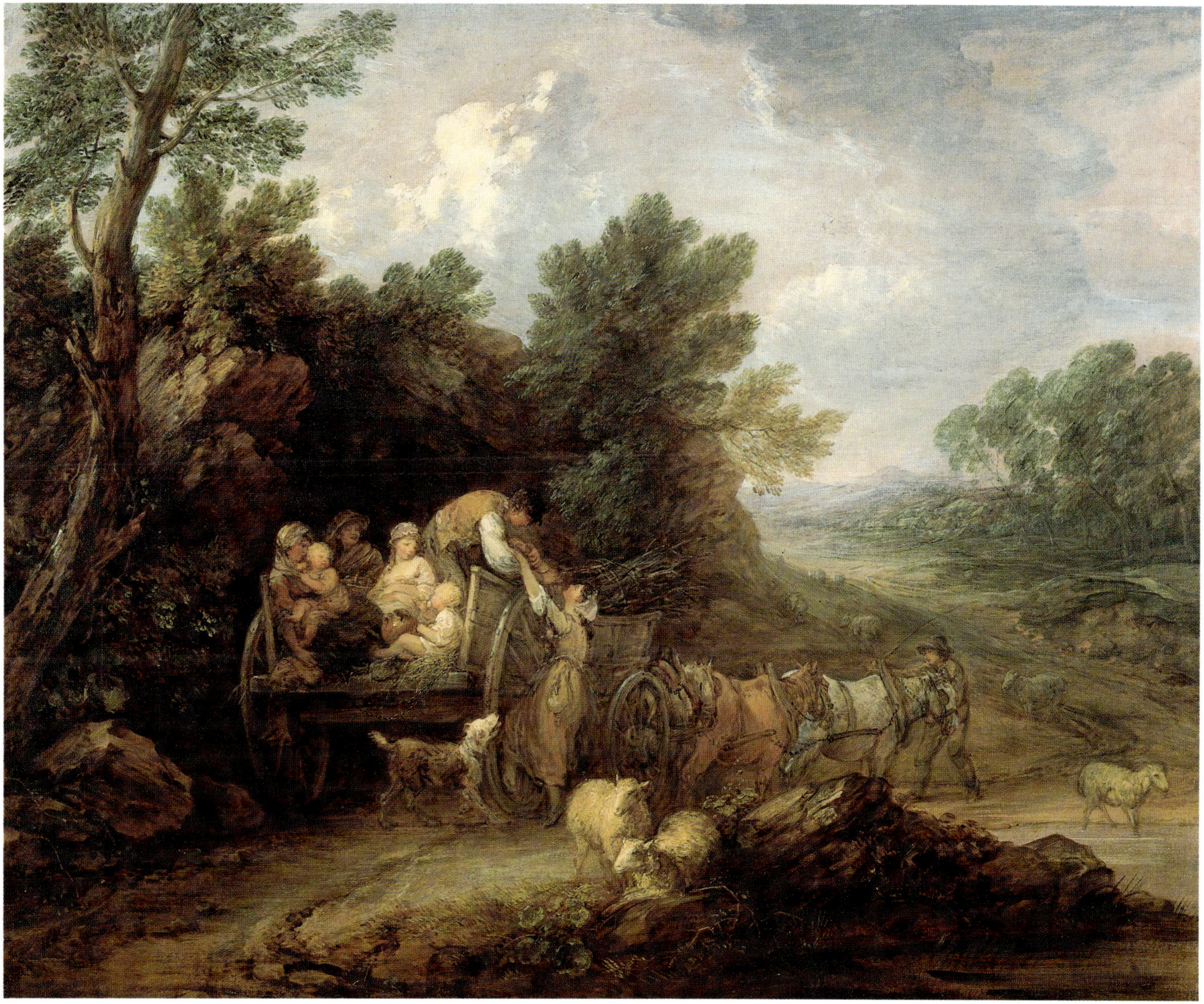

Plate II (cat. 2). Gainsborough, *The Harvest Wagon*, 1784/5
Art Gallery of Ontario, Toronto

"One of my best compositions": The Barber *Harvest Wagon*

Paul Spencer-Longhurst

". . . we must jogg on and be content with the jingling of the Bells, only d-mn it I hate a dust, the Kicking up of a dust, and being confined *in Harness* to follow the track, whilst others ride in the waggon, under cover, stretching their Legs in the straw at Ease, and gazing at Green Trees & Blue skies without half my Taste, that's damn'd hard".[1]

The Harvest Wagon at the Barber Institute of Fine Arts forms a watershed in the artistic career of Thomas Gainsborough. It confirms him as a mature landscapist of dazzling virtuosity; it marks him at a high moment of admiration for the exemplars of old master landscape, notably Rubens. As a figure painter it catches him at his most monumental and declamatory while his role as a portraitist emerges through the inclusion of at least one of his daughters as a model. The Barber *Harvest Wagon* was painted at a time of professional recognition for Gainsborough, when having been resident in Bath with no permanent London base for almost ten years he was invited to become a Founding Member of the Royal Academy, which received its charter in December 1768, eighteen months or so after the painting was completed.

It is almost certain that *The Harvest Wagon* was shown in 1767 at the Society of Artists of Great Britain, the Academy's predecessor and rival. Gainsborough exhibited both landscapes and portraits at their 'Great Room' in Spring Gardens, Pall Mall, from 1761 until 1768, after which he transferred his allegiance to the Academy. His landscape of 1767 was catalogued merely as *A Landskip and Figures*, but the foremost critic of the day, Horace Walpole, (cats. 26 and 27) referred to it in his annotated catalogue in these terms: "This landscape is very rich, the group of figures delightfully managed and the horses well drawn, the distant hill is one tint too dark".[2] Of Gainsborough's contemporary landscapes, it is *The Harvest Wagon* which this description most accurately fits. Another, anonymous, critic said of the same landscape: "The trees are hard and the sky too blue".[3] This would be more difficult to apply to *The Harvest Wagon*, at least as it now appears, were it not that the indigo pigment which Gainsborough used to paint his sky is prone to fading.[4]

There is a tradition that the artist exhibited *The Harvest Wagon* at the Academy exhibition of 1771, along with *Rocky Wooded Landscape with Rustic Lovers*, which remained its pendant for many years (cat. 14).[5] Gainsborough himself described the untitled landscapes which he had been preparing for the exhibition that year as "the best I ever did"[6] and Walpole characterised them as "very good but too little finished" – a remark that might well be applied to areas of *The Harvest Wagon*.[7] In any case, the painting was known to the public by 1774 at the latest as Francis Wheatley used and adapted Gainsborough's composition for his own *Harvest Wagon* (cat. 15), which is signed and dated that year. The lack of further recorded comment on Gainsborough's painting may reasonably suggest that it was not widely noticed. Assuredly it was not sold at either exhibition, for it remained in Gainsborough's own possession until he left Bath in 1774, when he gave it to his friend, the public carrier and local worthy, Walter Wiltshire.

Gainsborough's development as a landscapist underwent several transformations before the late 1760s. From his origins in East Anglia he acquired a fascination with the particularities of the Suffolk landscape and its inhabitants which never entirely deserted him, and which permeates his early landscapes, such as *Landscape with Country Wagon* (cat. 3). These works are interfused with the influence of seventeenth-century Dutch landscapists such as Jan Wijnants, Jacob van Ruisdael and Meyndert Hobbema, with whose work Gainsborough was familiar in East Anglian collections and through the medium of prints. According to a contemporary, "the first master he studied was Wynants, whose thistles and dock leaves he frequently introduced into his early pictures. The next was Ruysdale, but his colouring is less sombre . . .".[8] Evidence of Gainsborough's continuing fascination with his Netherlandish predecessors is to be found in the copies he still occasionally made of their paintings as late as the 1780s (cat. 23).

After his return to Sudbury in 1748 and establishment in Ipswich in 1752 the scope and physical dimensions of his landscapes widened markedly, and by the middle years of

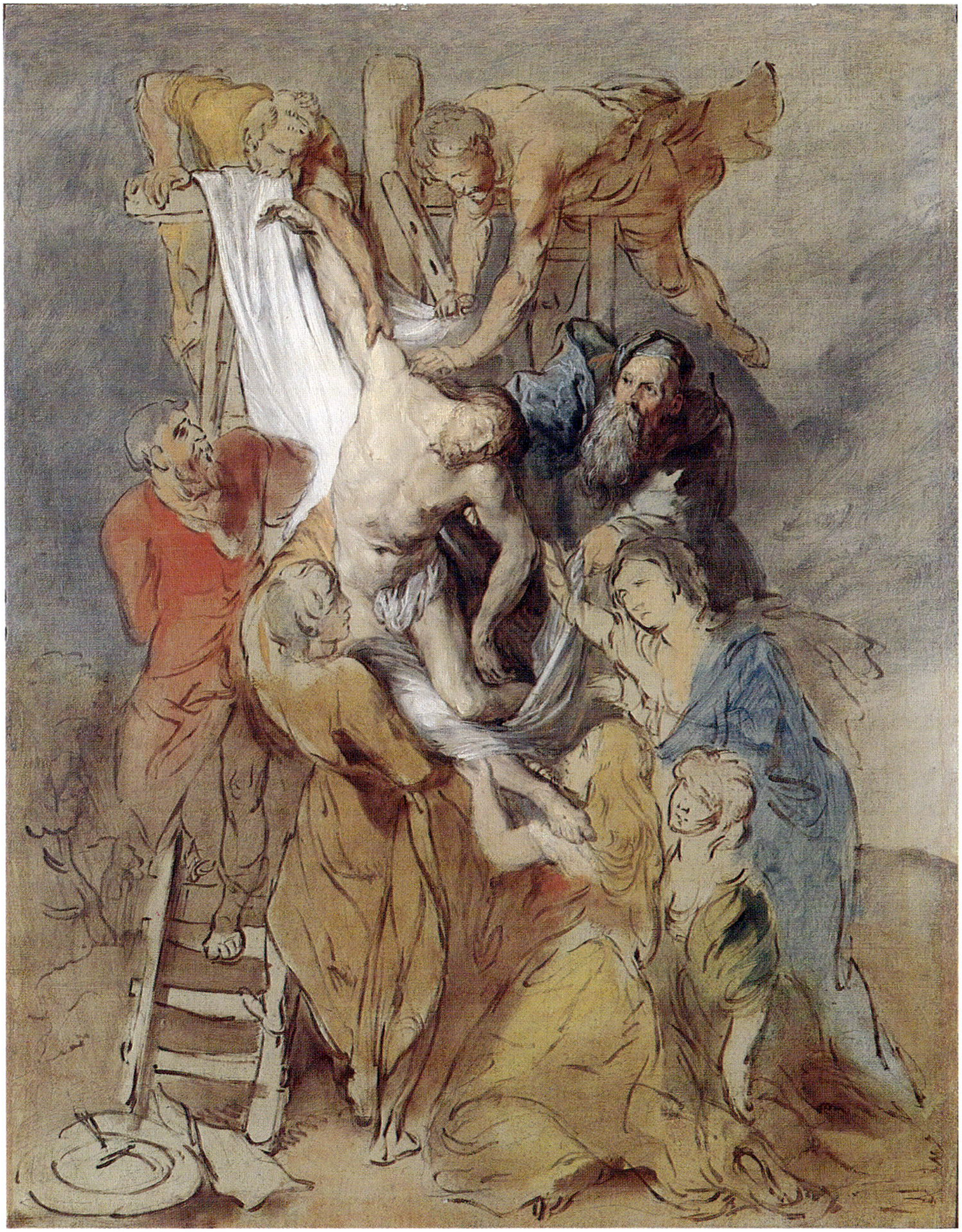

Plate III (cat. 8).
Gainsborough (after Rubens), *The Descent from the Cross*,
Private Collection, on loan to the Ashmolean Museum, Oxford

the decade there is a rococo feel in many of them, deriving from the influence of his French or Francophile contacts in London, Hubert François Gravelot (1699–1773) and Francis Hayman (1708–1776). Frequently featuring amorous rustic themes, they have been described by John Hayes as "a down-to-earth Anglicised equivalent of the sophisticated pastoral gallantry of Boucher or Fragonard".[9] There is still much of the French rococo style in the feathery trees of the Barber *Harvest Wagon*, and of gallic *galanterie* in its idyllic setting and the attention paid to the the girl mounting the wagon by her rustic beau. However, Gainsborough's move to Bath in 1759 effected a further and more significant transformation through the opportunity which it afforded him of studying major collections of old master paintings in the locality, notably those at Corsham, Bowood, Longford Castle, Stourhead and Wilton. In visits to such houses, often to paint portraits, he was able to absorb deeply the influence of Claude, Rubens and Van Dyck.

Gradually Gainsborough began to introduce fewer isolated motifs into his landscapes and his figures were given greater prominence, and were frequently spotlit (cat. 6). In the early 1760s he began to work by candlelight in a search for more unity, breadth and chiaroscuro. This was the moment when his nostalgia for the countryside and the settled ways of its people first emerged in pictures of peasants travelling to or from market, all of which share a highly sensitive evocation of mood and atmosphere. They include masterpieces such as *Going to Market* (cat. 13), *The Road from Market* (c. 1767–8, Toledo Museum of Art, Ohio)[10] and *Peasants going to Market: Early Morning* (c. 1773, formerly Royal Holloway College, Egham).[11] The bucolic lovers of the 1750s were by the mid-1760s yielding to more sophisticated and idyllic figures culminating in those in the Barber *Harvest Wagon*. At the very moment when the artist was working on this painting he was nurturing an intense enthusiasm for Rubens, whose baroque figure groupings, broadness of handling and dramatic use of double lighting assumed a special appeal for him. Under this influence Gainsborough lightened his palette, loosened his touch and endowed his subjects with increasing vigour, richness of tint and boldness of effect.

It did not prevent him, however, from continuing to give many of his landscapes the pervasive sunset glow and other compositional features of Claude (cats. 10 and 11). In this Gainsborough was very much a man of his time, for Claude was the prime inspiration of contemporaries such as John Wootton (c. 1682–1764), George Lambert (1700–1765) and Richard Wilson (1714–1782). His paintings were increasingly sought after by collectors[12] and there was much interest in his drawings, indicated by the publication of prints after them. Arthur Pond and Charles Knapton included Claude among their etched series of old master drawings published between 1732 and 1736. In 1777 there appeared the two volumes of etchings by Richard Earlom after Claude's *Liber Veritatis*, then in the collection of the Duke of Devonshire. A major aspect of Claude's appeal was the idealism of his landscapes. As Reynolds put it, "Claude Lorrain . . . was convinced, that taking nature as he found it seldom produced beauty. His pictures are a composition of the various draughts which he had previously made from various beautiful scenes and prospects".[13] Parallels exist here with Gainsborough's own working methods. Like Claude he seems to have mainly drawn individual motifs from nature which he then combined or translated into painted landscapes through the medium of his own imagination. There are marked Claudean characteristics in the Barber *Harvest Wagon*, most obviously the pastoral nature of the subject and the compositional device of framing the distant landscape with groups of trees; yet, in the treatment of the lighting, the bravura brushwork and the handling of the sky it is the influence of Rubens which is stronger.

Within a year of painting *The Harvest Wagon*, Gainsborough wrote to his friend, the actor David Garrick, "I could wish you to call *upon any pretence*, any day after next Wednesday at the Duke of Montagu, because you'd see the Duke and Duchess in my *last* manner; but not as if you thought anything of mine worth that trouble, only to see his Grace's Landskip of Rubens, and the 4 Vandykes whole length in his Grace's dressing-room".[14] The Rubens in question was *The Watering Place* (National Gallery, London), a work which, a decade later, was to inspire direct homage from Gainsborough in his own painting of the same title (National Gallery, London). This he exhibited at the Royal Academy in 1777 where it was described by Walpole as "in the style of Rubens, and by far the finest

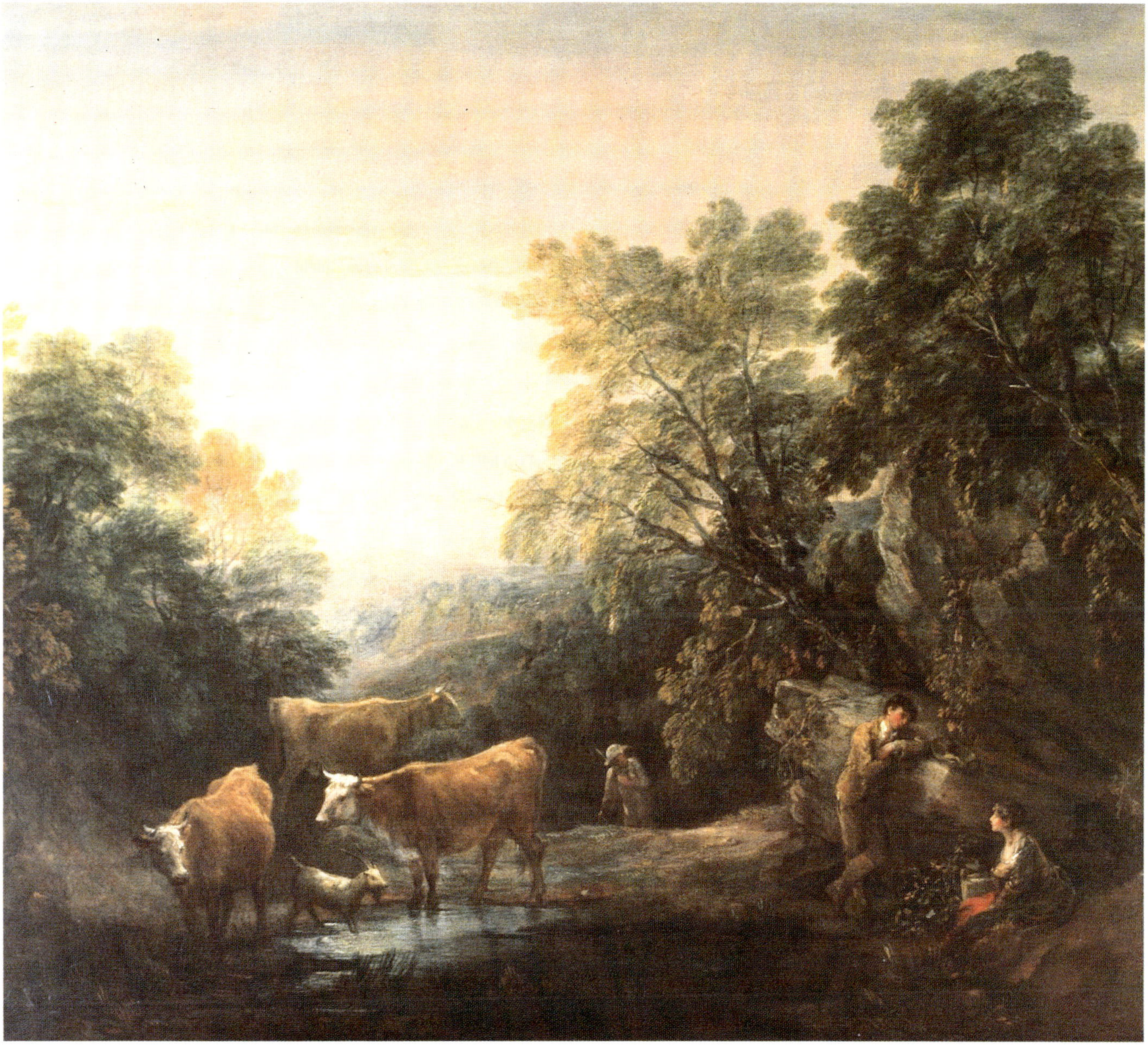

Plate IV (cat. 14). Gainsborough, *Rocky Wooded Landscape with Rustic Lovers*
Private Collection, United Kingdom

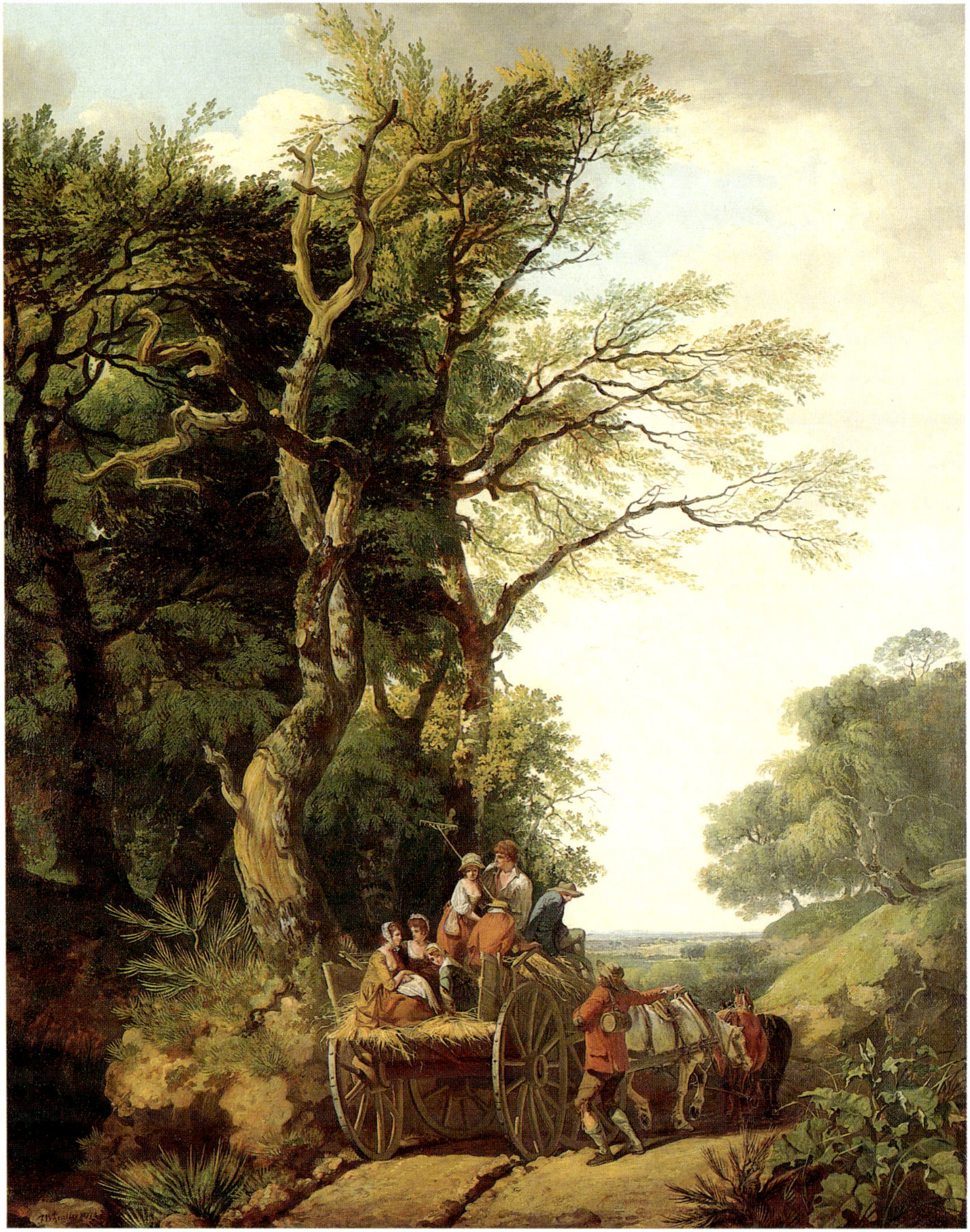

Plate V (cat. 15).
Francis Wheatley,
The Harvest Wagon,
City of Nottingham
Museums, Castle
Museum and Art
Gallery

landscape ever painted in England, and equal to the great masters".[15] There were other landscapes by or attributed to Rubens with which Gainsborough was familiar in the 1760s. Two paintings hung at Nuneham Park, Oxfordshire, home of the Harcourt family, with whom the artist had contact at Bath in 1758-9. One of these (cat. 16) was a copy of *The Mired Cart*, of which the primary version (Hermitage, St Petersburg) had been purchased by Sir Robert Walpole and hung at Houghton Hall, less than sixty miles from Gainsborough's native Sudbury. Two further Rubens landscapes were in the collection of Earl Camden, a patron of the artist at Bath;[16] and a replica of *A Shepherd with his Flock in a Woody Landscape* (National Gallery, London) was by 1758 in the collection of the Earl of Pembroke at Wilton, where Gainsborough spent a week in 1763.[17] Far more accessible, however, were engravings after Rubens (cats. 17 and 18). In Gainsborough's own collection of about fifty paintings, only two were attributed to Rubens, of which neither were landscapes,[18] and there is no record of his ever having copied a Rubens landscape. He did, however, make a magnificent copy of Rubens's *Descent from the Cross* (cat. 8), working from the engraving by Lucas Vorsterman (cat. 9) but almost certainly inspired by the modello (fig. 3), then at Corsham Court, about ten miles from Bath. Stylistically these undated copies belong to the 1760s.

The legitimacy of representing a harvest wagon or hay cart in a grand manner may well have been suggested to Gainsborough by his knowledge of Rubens, in whose landscapes such vehicles frequently appear. The motif is conspicuous, for example, in *The Return from Harvest* (Palazzo Pitti, Florence), which was engraved by Schelte Adamsz. Bolswert about 1635–40 and again by François Vivares in 1775. Similar wagons may be seen standing next to hayricks in the *Landscape with Rainbow* (Wallace Collection, London) and in Bolswert's engraving of the now-lost *Harvest Scene with Rainbow*. In *Summer* (Royal Collection, Windsor Castle) and *Autumn Landscape with a View of Het Steen* (National Gallery, London) a two-wheeled farm-cart laden with produce makes a prominent appearance. This, too, was a motif frequently used by Gainsborough, culminating in *The Market Cart* (cat. 24). Rubens's small panel *Evening: Countrywoman driving a Cart* (Wolfgang Burchard Collection) belonged in Gainsborough's day to John Hunter, F.R.S., one of his medical advisers,[19] and may have inspired his *Country Cart crossing a Ford* (c. 1782–4, Christchurch Mansion, Ipswich).

Gainsborough was a countryman by birth and upbringing, so in any event it is hardly surprising that country vehicles going about their business should feature at an early date in his landscapes. As a principal subject, the motif is first to be seen in the small *Landscape with Country Wagon* (cat. 3). About 1756–7, the artist adumbrated the motif of a family travelling home in *A Wooded Landscape with Peasants in a Country Wagon*.[20] In *Sunset: Carthorses drinking at a Stream* (Tate Gallery, London), painted about the time of his move to Bath, he developed the theme into an elegiac celebration of the end of the day's labour for animals and peasants alike. By the mid-1760s he was using drawings to experiment with the setting of such carts in woodland glades, sometimes employing the medium of watercolour (cat. 30).

At this period, Gainsborough was also becoming fascinated with the ideas of the nascent Picturesque movement, not least because they accorded with his own predisposition towards ruggedness, irregularity, intricacy and chiaroscuro. Of the writers on Picturesque theory over the last three decades of the eighteenth century, Gainsborough, as a man who is believed to have read little,[21] is most likely to have been influenced by the one he knew personally, Sir Uvedale Price (1747–1829). Price, who published his *Essay on the Picturesque* during the decade following Gainsborough's death, had become a friend of the artist as a youth more than thirty years earlier. The two men made sketching tours and viewed collections together in and around Bath, which must have helped form their ideas concerning the qualities of picturesqueness in landscape. A landscape attributed to Van Dyck, which Price acquired on his Grand Tour in 1767–8, is said to have been "a great favourite with Gainsborough".[22] Later Price must surely have had Gainsborough in mind when he wrote of the picturesqueness of "rough banks that often enclose a bye-road or a hollow lane".[23] Irregular and asymmetrical form coupled with *non-finito* technique are essential elements of the Picturesque aesthetic and a staple in

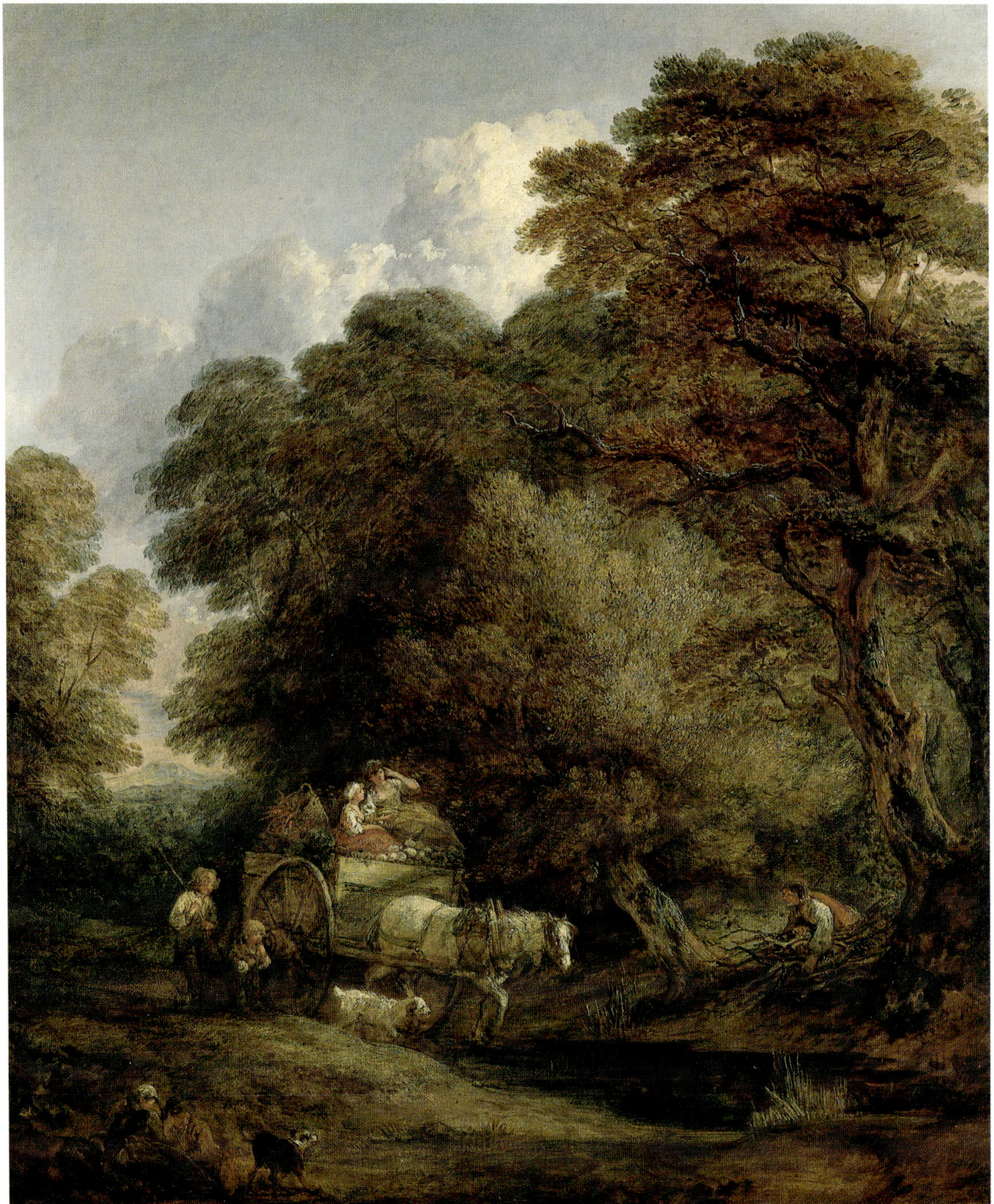

Plate VI (cat. 24).
Gainsborough,
The Market Cart,
The Trustees of the
National Gallery,
London

Gainsborough's landscapes. Nowhere are they better exemplified than in the old horses, which he frequently drew, and even modelled in clay (cat. 42). Often seen with their drovers or riders, they appear from the mid-1750s, notably in *Peasant with Two Horses: Haycart Behind* (fig. 2), and the study of an old grey horse in harness (Tate Gallery, London)[24] whose uneven form and lighting is echoed by those of the synthetically craggy tree on which it rests its head. A prominent feature of the Barber *Harvest Wagon* is the restless grey horse, restrained with difficulty in the very centre of the painting. Its position and pose are far more assertive than in the Toronto version. Edward Finden in his *Royal Gallery of British Art* (cat. 40) relates how Gainsborough, during his visits to Walter Wiltshire's country estate at Shockerwick, "often mounted an old grey horse, which recommended itself to the painter by its docility as well as by its rough, picturesque appearance. The horse became a great favourite of the artist, for when he was engaged with his pencil it would graze quietly by him and often furnished a subject to be introduced in the sketch. So attracted did he become to the animal that it somewhat piqued the family to perceive that whenever he left Shockerwick he appeared to feel more regret in abandoning the horse than in quitting their society. He offered to purchase it, but, though Mr Wiltshire refused to sell it he gladly presented it to the painter, who rode his acquisition to London. Not to be outdone in courtesy Gainsborough painted the picture [...] and presented it with grateful acknowledgement to Mr Wiltshire".[25] This story was confirmed by J. H. Anderdon, who, when at Bath, made the acquaintance of John Wiltshire, the carrier's son, who told him that the grey horse was the one that Gainsborough

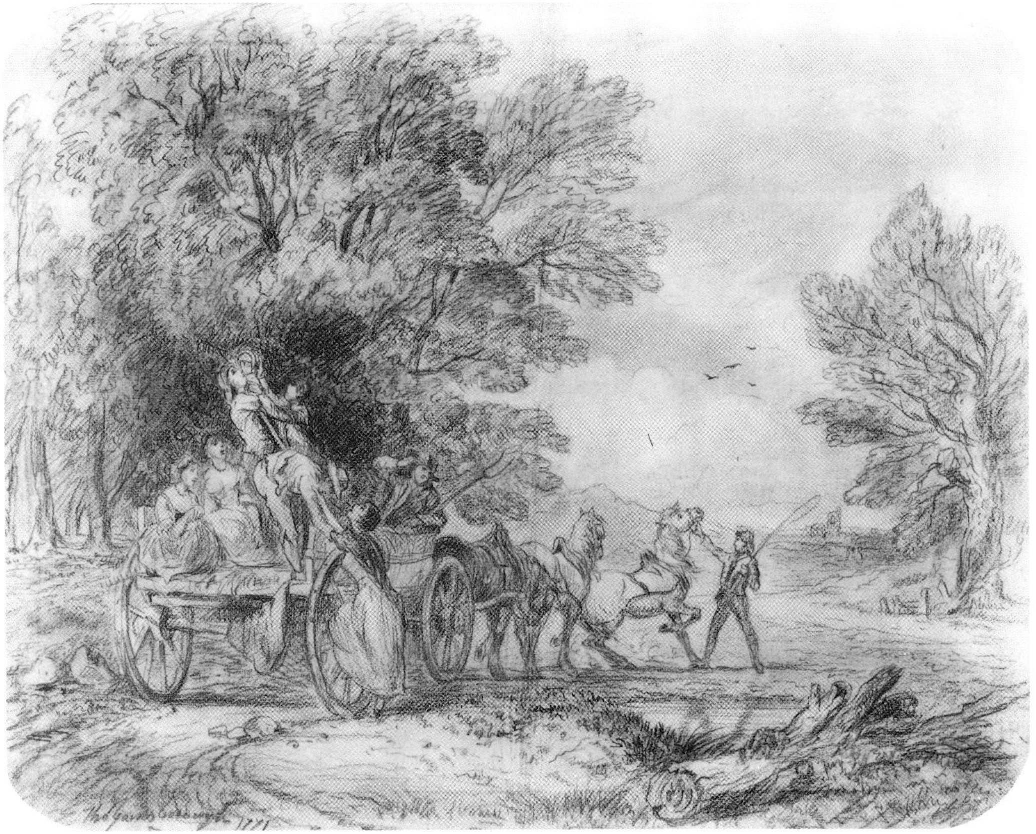

Fig. 1 Formerly attributed to Gainsborough, *The Harvest Wagon,* black chalk on paper, 406 × 540 mm, inscribed and dated lower left: *Tho Gainsborough 1771* Unlocated, formerly Dr. Sigmund Samuel, Toronto

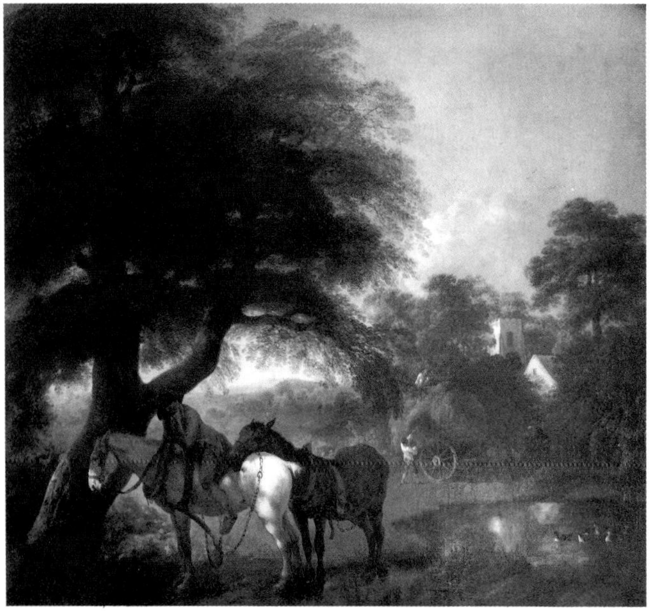

Fig. 2 Gainsborough, *Peasant with Two Horses: Haycart Behind* 1755, oil on canvas, 92.1 × 102.2 cm, signed: *TG*
The Marquess of Tavistock, Woburn Abbey

had been accustomed to ride, and that he took it with him when he removed to London in the summer of 1774. After trying vainly to induce the carrier to accept fifty guineas for the animal he sent him the picture instead, adding "Because I think this is one of my best compositions I send it to a gentleman who has vastly contributed to my happiness".[26] The leading horse in *The Harvest Wagon* hardly seems docile, even though its companions are very much in the mould of the Picturesque, with their rough and broken-down appearance. Yet all three are the fruit of careful observation by an artist who owned a copy of George Stubbs's *The Anatomy of the Horse*, just published in 1766. The heroic stance which Gainsborough gave to the drover who restrains the leading horse seems inspired by classical sculpture – *The Horse Tamers*, in the Piazza del Quirinale, Rome. Reproductions of these two monumental groups were enthusiastically admired in England, especially after the publication of J. H. Fuseli's translation of Winckelmann, *Reflections on the Painting and Sculpture of the Greeks*, in 1765. By alluding to them Gainsborough was demonstrating the versatility of landscape while responding, perhaps facetiously, to the insistence of Reynolds on the supremacy of ancient sculpture as source material for contemporary artists.[27]

Carts and wagons did not disappear from the artist's work after his move to London in 1774. In *Landscape with Figures in a Country Cart* of 1777–8[28] a two-wheeled cart carrying a girl, a pitcher and a basket disappears over the top of a rocky outcrop. Such a cart, also containing produce and a girl, is seen from the front in a drawing inscribed 1778.[29] A similarly orientated cart was used several times in the late 1770s by the artist, usually in combination with peasants and a cottage nestled among trees.[30] In *The Farmer's Cart* Gainsborough experimented with the motif of a farm-cart seen from behind and heading for a gap in the trees in very much the same way as the Barber *Harvest Wagon*.[31] This was a preparatory study for his print of the same subject (cat. 37).

During the last decade of his life, he returned to painting carts in extensive and dramatic landscapes. It is within the context of this revived interest that the genesis of the Toronto *Harvest Wagon* must be set. In the mid-1780s he painted *A Cart receding down a Woody Lane*, probably connected with a contemporary chalk and wash reprise of the earlier farm-cart theme.[32] Later in the decade came the magnificent *Country Cart crossing a Ford* (Christchurch Mansion, Ipswich)[33] and, as a glorious culmination in the winter of 1786, *The Market Cart* (cat. 24). In the latter the monumentality of design makes it a fitting comparison to the Toronto *Harvest Wagon*, and together these paintings may be seen as the apogee of Gainsborough's handling of this theme.

The Barber *Harvest Wagon* was executed at the mid point of Gainsborough's residence in Bath, when the majority of his time was taken up with portraiture rather than landscape. In this respect he was the victim of his own success, and indeed, became so busy that in 1767 he had to excuse the delay in delivery of portraits to one of his clients.[34] The patronage of wealthy and fashionable visitors to the spa town, however, translated him to the front rank of national attention. Benefiting from the influence of Van Dyck imbibed at the great houses in the vicinity, he began to produce stunning full-length portraits such as *Viscountess*

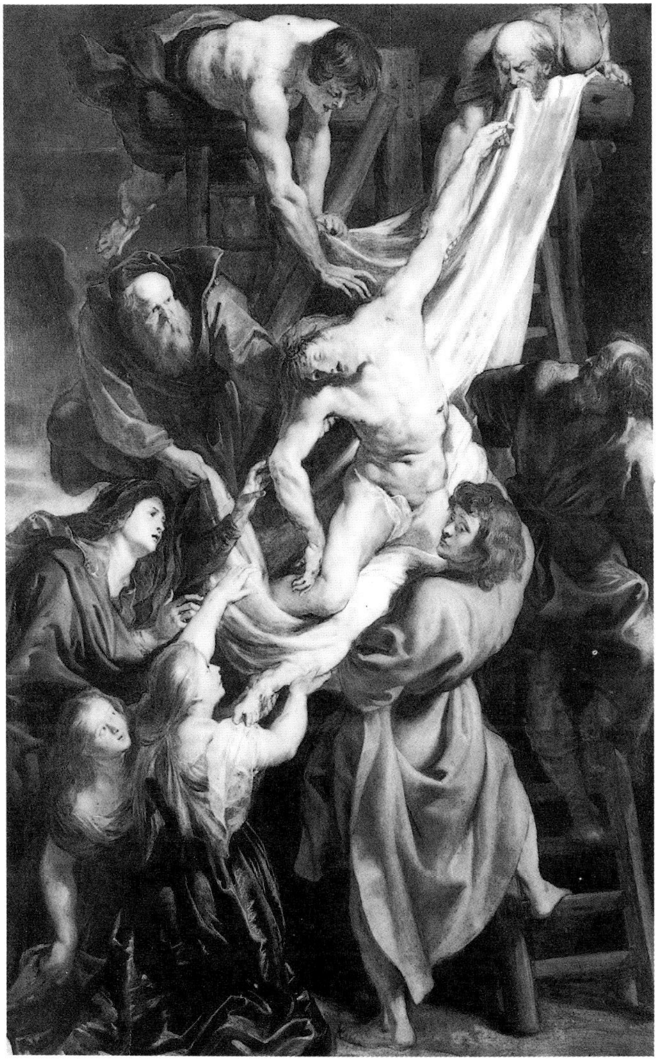

Fig. 3 Peter Paul Rubens, *The Descent from the Cross*, 1611, oil on panel, 115.2 × 76.2 cm, Courtauld Institute Galleries, London

Molyneux (Walker Art Gallery, Liverpool), exhibited in 1769 at the first Royal Academy exhibition.[35] Such masterpieces, however, took time, which Gainsborough increasingly came to resent. If portraiture was his profession, landscape, as he said, was his pleasure. Yet during these late Bath years, he was working at portraits full stretch, "daubing away for the exhibition". He protested against this state of affairs to his friend, the composer and amateur artist, William Jackson of Exeter: "I'm sick of Portraits and wish very much to take my Viol da Gamba and walk off to some sweet Village when I can paint Landskips and enjoy the fag End of Life in quietness and ease".[36] Some years after Gainsborough's death, the painter and critic, Prince Hoare, wrote that he was ". . . so disgusted at the blind preference paid to his powers of portraiture that, for many years of his residence at Bath he regularly shut up all his landscapes in the back apartments of his house, to which no common visitors were admitted".[37] Certainly, his reputation among the run of visitors to Bath was based on portraiture, as a brief mention in the letters of the Rev. John Penrose, written to his family from Bath in the years 1766–1767, makes clear: "From the P[ump] R[oom] we went to see Gainsborough's Portraits, among which was one of Lady Waldegrave; no such flaming beauty in my eyes".[38]

Even during his London years, the landscapes were ignored by potential patrons. The painter, William Beechey, relates how they "stood ranged in long lines from his hall to his painting room, and they who came to sit for him for their portraits . . . rarely deigned to honour them with a look as they passed them".[39] Limited recognition was forthcoming from fellow painters, like Thomas Jones (1742–1803), who recalled that at the beginning of his own career, "there was Lambert, & Wilson, & Zuccarelli, & Gainsborough, & Barret, & Richards, & Marlow in full possession of the Landscape business".[40] This nebulous alliance showed brief promise of assuming some coherent form, when, in the late 1760s William, Lord Shelburne commissioned Gainsborough, Wilson and Barret to paint masterpieces of landscape for his country house, Bowood. Gainsborough's contribution to this project, which was "intended to lay the foundation of a school of British landscapes"[41] was *The Road from Market* (Toledo Museum of Art, Ohio).

The predominance of portraiture in Gainsborough's oeuvre rested largely on its financial rewards, whereas the patronage of landscape was irregular and unreliable. His own dedication to landscape, however, was established from the beginning. He was described in his early London years as "only a landscape painter, and merely as such he must have starved – he did not sell six pictures a year".[42] In the 1750s he is known to have secured a few landscape commissions, eg. an overmantel of *Landguard Point and Fort* from Philip Thicknesse in 1753 and a river scene with cattle watering and a ferry boat from Thomas Spencer of Hart Hall, Suffolk.[43] In 1755 came the commission for two decorative overmantels from the Duke of Bedford (fig. 2), while the dealer, Panton Betew, handled smaller landscapes and drawings. Most of them however, were acquired either by friends, like the musician, Carl Friedrich Abel, or by patrons who, like Sir William St Quintin, had become friends. In 1766, Sir William paid £43-11s-6d for *Wooded Landscape with Country Wagon, Milkmaid and Drover* (cat. 6). *Peasants going to Market, Early Morning* was bought in 1773 by Henry Hoare, Gainsborough's banker. Among his Bath associates, Ralph Allen, of Prior Park, who owned the Bath stone quarries, possessed at least one small landscape by Gainsborough[44] and Dr. Rice Charlton, Gainsborough's physician, owned no fewer than six, including a copy after his own landscape by 'Bout and Boudewyns'.[45] Nevertheless, with the exception of *Rocky Wooded Upland Landscape* (fig. 6), commissioned by the Prince of Wales, much of the artist's output was either given away, like the Barber *Harvest Wagon*, or remained on his hands.

During the six-year period immediately preceding the Barber *Harvest Wagon* Gainsborough painted only a dozen or so landscapes, apart from backgrounds in portraits. He made many drawings, however, during expeditions to the surrounding countryside with friends, such as the miniaturist, Ozias Humphrey or the young Uvedale Price. Places visited included Claverton, Warleigh, Weston, and Shockerwick Park, the home of Walter Wiltshire. Wiltshire was a man of considerable local eminence who had made a fortune from his successful carrier service which operated from a warehouse in Broad Street, Bath, to the White Swan on Holborn Bridge, London. Gainsborough used his 'flying waggon' to transport his paintings for exhibition in the capital. During the year 1772, for example, he entrusted Wiltshire with no fewer than fourteen of his pictures.[46] Wiltshire had inherited the manor of Shockerwick and later commissioned John Wood the elder to build an "elegant house of Bath stone in a warm, pleasant situation, with fine gardens". Shockerwick became the centre of a social circle which included Ralph Allen, Christopher Anstey, author of *The Bath Guide*, and the actor, James Quin. For Gainsborough it became a favourite location, not only for the stimulating company of such men but also for its landscape setting. His attachment to it is most graphically described by Finden, who was told by John Wiltshire how ". . . the painter frequently visited, and every spot about the hospitable mansion furnished him with studies. He often sketched parts of the house, the rocks about Hampton Cliffs[47] and the picturesque old trees and green lanes, and thereby so far made them his own that a thousand things in Shockerwick and its vicinity are recognised in his pictures. A flourishing old tree in the park still bears the name of 'Gainsborough's Elm'. In short he found there nearly all the materials which he required for his pictures, and made his studies of waggons, horses, etc".[48] A number of these drawings survive, identified with greater or lesser degrees of certainty, but there are few which are direct studies for finished landscape paintings, and none for the Barber *Harvest Wagon*. In this painting the sole hint of a particular location is the church tower to the right of the distant landscape, which is now only vaguely defined owing to damage sustained in the 1940s.[49] Rather it is for the group of figures and the wagon that drawings do survive (cats. 28 and 29).

A large-scale, active figure-group is an exceptional phenomenon in Gainsborough's landscapes before 1780. Gainsborough's thoughts on the function and status of figures in his landscapes are summarised in a letter written probably in the very year when the Barber *Harvest Wagon* was exhibited. A landscape, he believed, should never be "fill'd with History, or any figures but such as fill a place (I won't say stop a Gap) or [. . .] create a little business for the Eye to be drawn from the Trees in order to return to them with more glee".[50] That figures should appear so prominently at precisely this moment in the Barber *Harvest Wagon* suggests that the artist had a particular reason. Very probably this was a desire to assert the validity of landscape as a genre against the exclusive claims of history painting, promulgated at the Royal Academy. Gainsborough's complex arrangement of girls and men in *The Harvest Wagon* gave status to an already majestic scene conceived in the grand manner. If the picture was indeed exhibited at the Royal Academy of 1771, references to the accepted canon of old masters, as advocated by Reynolds, would be the more appropriate. Indeed, it is conceivable that the Barber *Harvest Wagon* and *Rocky Wooded Landscape with Rustic Lovers* (cat. 14) were intended as demonstrations of Gainsborough's ability to paint in the manner of Rubens and Claude respectively. It was probably for this reason that Gainsborough used as inspiration *The Descent from the Cross* by Rubens (fig. 3). The noticeable discrepancy between the relative elegance of the women's costume and the drab but more realistic dress of the men may be explained in this context as both reflecting the contrasts in the Rubens *Descent from the Cross* and providing the minimum finery consistent with a landscape in the grand manner.

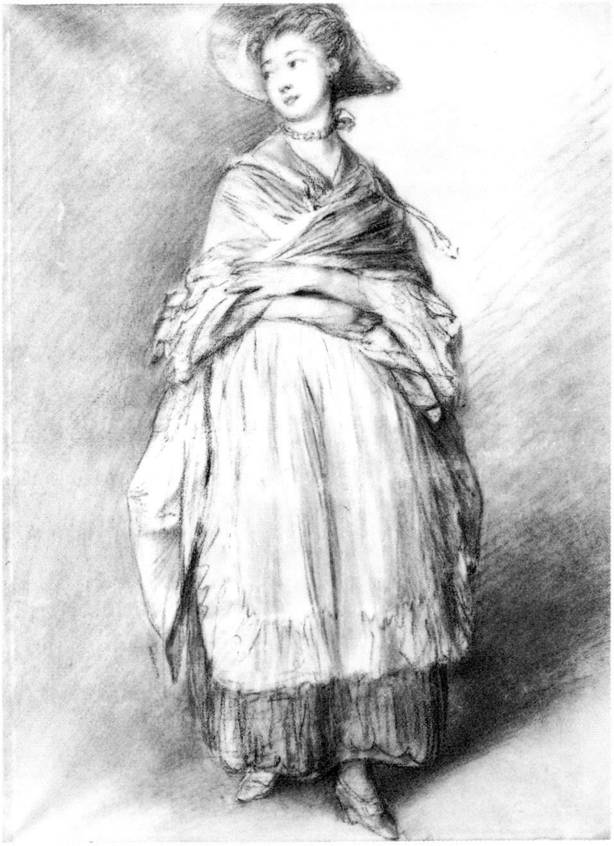

Fig. 4 Gainsborough, *Mary Gainsborough*, c. 1765–70, black chalk heightened with white on grey-green paper, 447 × 344 mm, The Trustees of the British Museum, London

In treating the theme of harvest Gainsborough was part of a tradition which stretches back to medieval books of hours and seasons of the year. In the eighteenth century, however, scenes of haymaking and harvest – there is some ambiguity as to which is intended in *The Harvest Wagon*[51] – began to emerge as a genre in British painting, for example in the work of Lambert and Stubbs.[52] The literature of the period is rich in georgic poetry, by, among others, John Gay, John Dyer and, pre-eminently, James Thomson.[53] Parallels can be drawn between these and Gainsborough's paintings, for example, his depiction of the vitality of country life and its representation in Gay's *Shepherd's Week*.[54] It is possible to construe *The Harvest Wagon* as an illustration of such poetry, and to ascribe the contrast between the rough 'clowns' and the attractive girls in it to the artist's response to such a contrast in *The Shepherd's Week*. Similarly, lines from Thomson's *Summer* may be applied to *The Harvest Wagon:* "The rustic youth, brown with meridian toil,/ Healthful and strong; full as the summer rose/ Blown by prevailing suns, the ruddy maid,/ Half naked, swelling at the sight, and all/ her kindled graces burning o'er her cheek".[55] It is also tempting to try to identify a geographical setting for *The Harvest Wagon* – whether on the road to Chippenham[56] or, in the case of the Toronto version, among the rocks at Wick or Hampton. Yet to do so is surely to miss the point. Poetry and topography were inspirations to Gainsborough, but his imagination took them as raw material and produced from them its own highly personal vision of nature.[57] In a letter to Lord Hardwicke, written about three years before the exhibition of the Barber *Harvest Wagon*, the artist declared, "with respect to *real Views* from Nature in this Country he has never seen any Place that affords a Subject equal to the poorest imitations of Gaspar or Claude [...] if his Lordship wishes to have anything tolerable of the name of G, the subject altogether as well as figures etc. must be of his own Brain".[58] *The Harvest Wagon* was a theme round which Gainsborough composed variations for most of his life. Its unique importance for him is demonstrated by his reprise of the Barber composition almost twenty years later, and its metamorphosis into the equally beautiful but very different *Harvest Wagon* now at Toronto.

1 Gainsborough, Letter to William Jackson of Exeter, 4th June 1772: Woodall, *Letters*, no. 56, p. 115.
2 A. Graves, *The Society of Artists of Great Britain*, London, 1907, p. 98.
3 Anon., *A Critical Examination of the Pictures*, London, 1767, p. 9.
4 On Gainsborough's use of indigo, see his undated letters of thanks to William Jackson [1768], Woodall, *Letters*, no. 53, p. 107, and no. 57, p. 117.
5 The Barber *Harvest Wagon* was stated to be one of the two landscapes exhibited there in the entry for lot 61 of the Henry J. Pfungst sale, Christie's, 15 June 1917. An unlocated drawing, formerly in the collection of Dr. Sigmund Samuel of Toronto, replicates *The Harvest Wagon* almost exactly (fig. 1). It is signed and dated 1771 but from photographic evidence seems weak and in a later style than Gainsborough's.
6 Letter to the Hon. Edward Stratford of 21 March 1771, Woodall, *Letters*, no. 79, p. 143.
7 A. Graves, *The Royal Academy of Arts*, III, London, 1907, p. 190.
8 The anonymous obituarist of *The Morning Chronicle*, quoted in exh. cat., London, Tate Gallery, *Thomas Gainsborough*, 1980–1, p. 76.
9 Ibid., p. 98.
10 Hayes, no. 89.
11 Hayes, no. 107.
12 This is confirmed by the evidence of picture sales over the century. In 1722, at the Duke of Portland's sale, three major Claudes were sold for £151, £200 and £280. In 1795 *The Enchanted Castle* (National Gallery, London), changed hands for £546. In 1799 William Beckford bought two examples, formerly in the Altieri collection, Rome, for £6,825. See the exh. cat., London, Tate Gallery, 1973, *Landscape in Britain c. 1750 – c. 1850*, p. 15.
13 Sir Joshua Reynolds, Discourse IV, Royal Academy 1771: *Discourses on Art*, ed. R. Wark, San Marino, 1959, pp. 69–70.
14 Letter to Garrick, n.d., but endorsed by Garrick as 1768; Woodall, *Letters*, no. 27, p. 67.
15 A. Graves, *The Royal Academy of Arts*, III, London, 1907, p. 191.
16 One was *Sunset: A Wagon Fording a Stream* (Museum Boymans-van Beuningen, Rotterdam); the other is untraced.
17 An undated letter to James Unwin [1763], Woodall, *Letters*, no. 86, p. 155, refers to the stay.
18 *Rubens's Wife* (unlocated) and *Two Monks' Heads* (Ashmolean Museum, Oxford). See [Tancred Borenius], 'Gainsborough's Collection of Pictures', *Burlington Magazine*, LXXXIV, May 1944, p. 109.
19 John Hunter sale, Christie's, 29 January 1794, lot 35.
20 Sotheby's, London, 19 November 1986, lot 87.
21 W. Jackson, *The Four Ages, together with Essays on Various Subjects*, 1798, p. 183: ". . . so far from writing, he scarcely ever read a book . . ." For an opposing view, see Marcia Pointon, 'Gainsborough and the Landscape of Retirement', *Art History*, II-4, December 1979, p. 442.
22 Uvedale Price sale, Sotheby's 3-4 May 1854, 2nd day, lot 279, cited in Hayes, p. 280, n. 137.
23 *An Essay on the Picturesque*, London, 1796, pp. 106–7.
24 Hayes, no. 51a.
25 Edward and William Finden, *The Royal Gallery of British Art*, 1843, unpaginated text.
26 According to Anderdon, cited in W. T. Whitley, unpublished addendum to *Thomas Gainsborough*, London, 1915, p. 40, "Mr [John] Wiltshire, who was an excellent and benevolent magistrate and an amiable man, told me this anecdote when I visited him in April, 1841".
27 In Discourse III, delivered at the Royal Academy in December 1770, Reynolds discussed "the great leading principles of the grand style" and recommended "a careful study of the works of the ancient sculptors, who, being indefatigable in the school of nature, have left models of that perfect form behind them, which an artist would prefer as supremely beautiful who had spent his whole life in that simple contemplation". (Reynolds, *Discourses on Art*, 1959, p. 45).
Gainsborough admitted that he thought Reynolds's Discourse IV of 1771 "amazingly clever, and cannot be too much admired [. . .] The truth of what he observes concerning Fresco, and the Great style, Mr G. is convinced of by what he has often heard [. . .] of the works of Raffaelle and Michael Angelo – But betwixt Friends Sir Joshua either forgets, or does not chuse to see that his Instruction is all adapted to form the History Painter, which he must know there is no call for in this country". (Woodall, *Letters*, no. 46, p. 95).
28 Hayes, no. 118.
29 Hayes, *Drawings*, no. 464.
30 For example Hayes, *Drawings*, no. 644, formerly in the collections of Dr. Monro and Francis Wheatley, now in the Smith College Museum of Art, Northampton, Mass.
31 Whitworth Art Gallery, Manchester; Hayes, *Drawings*, no. 407.
32 W. W. Spooner collection, Bath; Hayes, *Drawings*, no. 754.
33 Hayes, no. 144.
34 Woodall, *Letters*, no. 73, p. 135.
35 Waterhouse, no. 606. *Viscountess Molyneux* was mentioned as having attracted great attention at the exhibition by the *Evening Post*, 1–3 May, 1769, p. 427; and by other journals.
36 Letter to William Jackson, 4 June 1772: Woodall, *Letters*, no. 56, p. 115.
37 Prince Hoare, *Epochs of the Arts*, London, 1813, pp. 76–7.
38 B. Mitchell and H. Penrose, eds., *Letters from Bath 1766-1767 by the Rev. John Penrose*, Gloucester, 1983, p. 137.
39 Fulcher, p.116.
40 'Memoirs of Thomas Jones', 1769, in *Walpole Society*, XXXII, 1946–1948, pp. 19–20.
41 Quoted in Hayes, pp. 120 and 431.

42 Exh. cat., London, Tate Gallery, *Thomas Gainsborough* 1980-1, p. 19.
43 Hayes, nos. 37 and 56 respectively.
44 Hayes, no. 76.
45 Peeter Bout (1658–1719) and Adriaen Frans Boudewyns (1644–1711). The landscape is mentioned in a letter from Gainsborough to Charlton, dated 1779, cited in exh. cat., *Gainsborough in Bath*, Holburne Museum and Craft Centre, Bath, 1988, under no. 31. Also in Charlton's collection was *Landscape with a Woodcutter* (1762-3, Museum of Fine Arts, Houston, Texas; Hayes, no. 77).
46 Exh. cat., *Gainsborough in Bath*, Holburne Museum and Craft Study Centre, Bath, 1988, p. 35.
47 Hampton Rocks, above Bathampton, were one of the most dramatic locations in the vicinity of Bath.
48 Whitley, unpublished addendum to p. 40 of his *Thomas Gainsborough*, 1915.
49 Finden and Josey in their engravings (cats. 40 and 41) clearly show a church. It bears some resemblance to All Saints' Church, Weston.
50 Letter to William Jackson, 23 August [1767?]: Woodall, *Letters*, no. 49, p. 99.
51 The presence of pitchforks and rakes rather than sickles suggests haymaking whereas the ears of wheat or barley visible in the wagon seem to confirm that harvest is intended. The title of the picture has varied (see for example Josey's engraving, cat. 41).
52 An early instance is Lambert's *View of Leybourne Grange, Kent, with Haymakers in the Park* of 1737 (Anon. sale, Christie's, London, 14 July 1989, lot 52).
53 Gay's *Rural Sports* was published in 1713 and his *Shepherd's Week* in 1714. Dyer's *The Fleece* was published in 1757. The first complete edition of Thomson's *Seasons* appeared in 1730; revised editions came out in 1744 and 1746 and were frequently reprinted.
54 John Barrell, *The Dark Side of the Landscape*, Cambridge, 1980, pp. 54–65.
55 *Summer*, 1746 edition, lines 353–7.
56 E. and W. Finden, 1843, unpaginated text.
57 His practice of constructing models of landscapes is well known. One observer noted that he had "more than once sat by him of an evening, and seen him make models, or rather thoughts, for landscape scenery [. . .]. He would place cork or coal for his foregrounds, make middle grounds of sand and clay, bushes of mosses and lichens, and set up distant woods of broccoli". ('Ephraim Hardcastle' [W. H. Pyne], *Wine and Walnuts*, 2nd edition, II, London, 1824, p. 197).
58 Woodall, *Letters*, no. 42, pp. 87–91.

"The Prince's Taste": The Toronto *Harvest Wagon*

Janet M. Brooke

In his critique of the 1814 British Institution exhibition, which included the Barber and Toronto *Harvest Wagons*, William Hazlitt wrote that Gainsborough had "led the way to that masquerade style, which piques itself on giving the air of an Adonis to the driver of a hay-cart, and models the features of a milk-maid on the principles of the antique."[1] Hazlitt's remark captures – with an acuity few have equalled since – the distinctive character of Gainsborough's 'fancy pictures' and figural landscapes. For what he dismissed as the affectation of the most important landscape painter of the previous generation is the key to the understanding of those pictures: Gainsborough's distillation of the language of the grand manner into a meaningful idiom for his own time. Gainsborough's two versions of *The Harvest Wagon* must be seen in terms of that aspiration; indeed, close examination of the two pictures, alike in size and subject-matter – but little else – reveals for us its remarkable breadth, persistence and evolution over a twenty-year period.

Nothing is known of the circumstances prompting Gainsborough's reprise in 1784 of the *Harvest Wagon* theme, in the picture now at the Art Gallery of Ontario, Toronto (cat. 2). That he was conscious of reshaping the composition he had so brilliantly painted almost twenty years earlier can nevertheless be inferred. Gainsborough's preference for landscape painting over the portraiture by which he earned his living is well-known.[2] As with the 'rustic courtship' theme that he treated frequently in the 1760s and 1770s, the subject of peasants returning from the field or going to market is common to his landscapes, increasingly so from the 1770s onward. Yet rarely are his landscapes so close in composition and theme as the Barber and Toronto *Harvest Wagons*, one notable exception being the Iveagh Bequest *Going to Market* of c. 1768–71 (cat. 13) and the landscape of similar title painted c. 1773 formerly in the collection of Royal Holloway College, Egham.[3] Yet these two pictures are close in date and indeed belong, with the Barber *Harvest Wagon*, to a group of landscapes that included, as the artist himself acknowledged in 1771, "the best I ever did."[4] Indeed, his own regard for these pictures may provide the best explanation for his return to the composition many years later.

In his essay in this volume, Paul Spencer-Longhurst considers the Barber *Harvest Wagon* in the context of Gainsborough's Bath period and examines the emergent influence of Rubens during this time. He describes, in particular, what is surely one of the more remarkable examples of pictorial transposition in the history of art, namely Gainsborough's mutation of the central motif of Rubens's *Descent from the Cross* into a boisterous group of peasants in the back of a wagon (cat. 8).

As John Hayes has shown, Rubens's influence on Gainsborough was already a matter of critical record by 1778, when Bate-Dudley wrote that Gainsborough was "a competitor of Rubens ... in the peculiarly characteristic description of his landscapes."[5] Indeed, while the spiralling figural group in the Barber *Harvest Wagon* provides us with the most literal instance of this influence, it is clear that from the mid 1760s onwards, Gainsborough knew and admired Rubens's landscape paintings. They were popular among English collectors, and Horace Walpole's belief that "seldom that he practised it, Rubens was never greater than in landscape" should be regarded as authoritative for that time, and demonstrates already by the 1760s a critical shift from the influence of Claude: "the tumble of [Rubens's] rocks and trees, the deep shadows in his glades and glooms, the watery sunshine, and dewy verdure, show a variety of genius ... are not to be found in the inimitable but uniform glow of Claud Lorrain."[6] Among the several landscapes Gainsborough knew or could have seen were two versions of Rubens's *Mired Cart*, one in the collection of Viscount Harcourt at Nuneham (cat. 16) and the other, now at the Hermitage Museum, St. Petersburg, that was at Houghton in the collection of Walpole's father, Sir Robert, and sold to Catherine II of Russia in 1779. Two engravings of this composition (of which two additional copies are known[7]) – by John Browne in 1776 and by Schelte Adamsz. Bolswert from a portfolio of twenty-one prints after Rubens and Ertvelt (1635–40, cats. 17 and 18) – would have provided Gainsborough with additional access to this image.[8] Hayes has proposed a relationship between *The Mired Cart* and the Toronto *Harvest Wagon*,[9] and there is reason here to favour a print source over any of the painted versions of Rubens's composition. In his earlier quotation of the grouping from Rubens's *Descent from the Cross* in the Barber version, Gainsborough relied ultimately on Vorsterman's engraving (cat. 9), as is clear from his own painted copy of the same motif (cat. 8). Similarly, the reversed composition in the engravings after *The Mired Cart* (cats. 17 and 18) more clearly reveals the extent of Gainsborough's indebtedness to that image for the Toronto *Harvest Wagon*. As in the engraving, the action begins at the lower left. The wagon has moved closer to the centre of the composition than in the Barber version and is positioned with a strong downward tilt like the wagon in the engraving. The figure pushing his weight against the side of the vehicle in the Rubens composition is posed in the same way as the farm girl in both the Barber and Toronto pictures, and the large crooked tree to the left in the Toronto picture echoes that in the engraving. In both, the wagon and its inhabitants are grounded against a looming rocky extrusion that dominates the composition.

Hayes has described the Toronto *Harvest Wagon* composition as "perhaps the most fully Rubenesque to be found in Gainsborough's landscapes."[10] Indeed, for all the compositional similarities between the two *Harvest Wagons* on the one hand, and the Toronto version and the engravings after *The Mired Cart* on the other, the real differences between Gainsborough's two landscapes are differences in spirit. His reliance on Rubens has moved from mere appropriation to assimilation. Whereas the painterly language of the Barber *Harvest Wagon* remains firmly rooted in baroque and rococo French painting, the strategies of the Toronto canvas are fully Rubensian in the strong spotlighting of the figural group against dark masses to the upper left and lower right. Unlike the Barber version, where the landscape setting functions almost as a stage set for the figural group in the immediate foreground, the inhabitants of the Toronto composition are fully integrated into their environment. Finally, the thinness of Gainsborough's paint application, the summary execution of foliage as patterns of loops and the subtle rearrangement of the composition from predominately horizontal to diagonal have all been recognised as responses to Rubens's pervasive influence on Gainsborough's late work.[11]

The influence of Rubens's *Mired Cart* on Gainsborough should not blind us to the possibility of additional sources – both in spirit and form – for the Toronto *Harvest Wagon*. He had clearly absorbed the elegant pictorial language of Van Dyck's English portraits into his own portrait style and his admiration for that artist is recorded by Farington: "within a very short time of his death He talked of Vandyke, whose works He delighted in."[12] Despite the relationship we have described between the Toronto *Harvest Wagon* and Rubens's *Mired Cart*, there is an episodic quality to the narrative of this and other Rubens landscapes that is absent from Gainsborough's painting. Further, Rubens's compositions are usually structured laterally across the picture plane, while that of the *Harvest Wagon* sweeps in a strong diagonal from upper left to lower right. Closer structural analogies are to be found in Van Dyck's paintings, such as *Charles I on Horseback*, then in the Royal Collection (c. 1638, National Gallery, London), composed in much the same way, and the *Cupid and Psyche* of 1639–40, also painted while Van Dyck was in England (Royal Collection, Kensington Palace). This picture, in particular, is dominated by an elegant curved diagonal that is remarkably close to that of Gainsborough's composition. It is intriguing to speculate that Gainsborough may have known the *Cupid and Psyche*, for the year following the execution of the *Harvest Wagon*, he attempted (apparently uncommissioned) the only mythological subject of his career, *Diana and Actaeon* (unfinished, 1785, Royal Collection, Buckingham Palace) requiring the representation of female nudes in a wooded setting.[13]

As Hayes has noted, Gainsborough modelled the head of the bonneted figure seated in shadow in the wagon on Hogarth's *Shrimp Girl*, though in reverse (National Gallery, London).[14] The two lively mother and child groupings have a decidely Rubenesque air, and the closest comparison to the profile figure to the left is Rubens's singularly unmaternal female in his *Samson and Delilah* (National Gallery, London), whose head tilts forward and whose right arm drops loosely to her side in much the same way.

The motif of the wagon advancing away from the picture plane can be traced to Gainsborough's early career, in such works as the *Landscape with Country Wagon* of c. 1746–7 (cat. 3). Hayes suggests that it too may be derived from Rubens;[15] certainly it appears in seventeenth-century Flemish landscapes, including those of Rubens and Jan Brueghel the Elder and Younger. Unlike these precedents, or even Gainsborough's youthful work, a festive charm of distinctly eighteenth-century French flavour permeates both the Barber and Toronto *Harvest Wagons*. Albeit barely implied, the narrative in the two pictures is the return from the fields and labour's just rewards. Like the figures in the Kenwood *Going to Market* (cat. 13), these peasants are a well-scrubbed lot, graceful of pose and delicate of gesture, who might feel more at home in Boucher's elegant ribaldries and Pater's *fêtes galantes* than Rubens's kermesses.

In the Barber *Harvest Wagon*, labour's bounty has a bacchanalian cast, with two young men vying for a cider keg while the women look on or climb aboard. Thematic parallels to this bucolic revelry are found in contemporary French art, where the rustic is melded to the mythological as in, among many examples, Joseph-Charles Marin's terracotta relief of *The Triumph of Bacchus* (fig. 5). Indeed, a mythic mood permeates many of Gainsborough's figural landscapes that Waterhouse describes as "a poetic 'Arcadia' remote from the world of fashion and individualist endeavour to which Gainsborough's portrait sitters belong."[16] Marcia Pointon sees a relationship between these works and the philosophy of retirement – retreat from the city and society for the pleasures of country living – that was popular in English literary circles during the second half of the eighteenth century.[17] Certainly Gainsborough echoed its sentiment when he wrote: "... [I] wish very much to take my Viol da Gamba and walk off to some sweet Village when I can paint Landskips and enjoy the fag End of Life in quietness & ease."[18]

The wistfulness permeating Toronto's *Harvest Wagon* is of a different sort: serenity has taken the place of gay abandon. The keg is replaced by a water-jug, and the tipsy pyramid of seated and standing figures has become a solid massing of bodies barely extending above the protective enclosure of the vehicle. Most important, Gainsborough has introduced two infant children into the figural group. Lovingly attentive through touch and gaze, their mothers are rustic madonnas who impart a quasi-sacred tone to the narrative (see also cat. 35). This shift in mood is consistent with a general moralising trend in Gainsborough's late figural landscapes that is explicitly sentimental in the 'fancy pictures'. In this sense Gainsborough's later *Harvest Wagon* is better compared to *The Cottage Door* of 1780 (Henry E. Huntington Library and Art Gallery, San

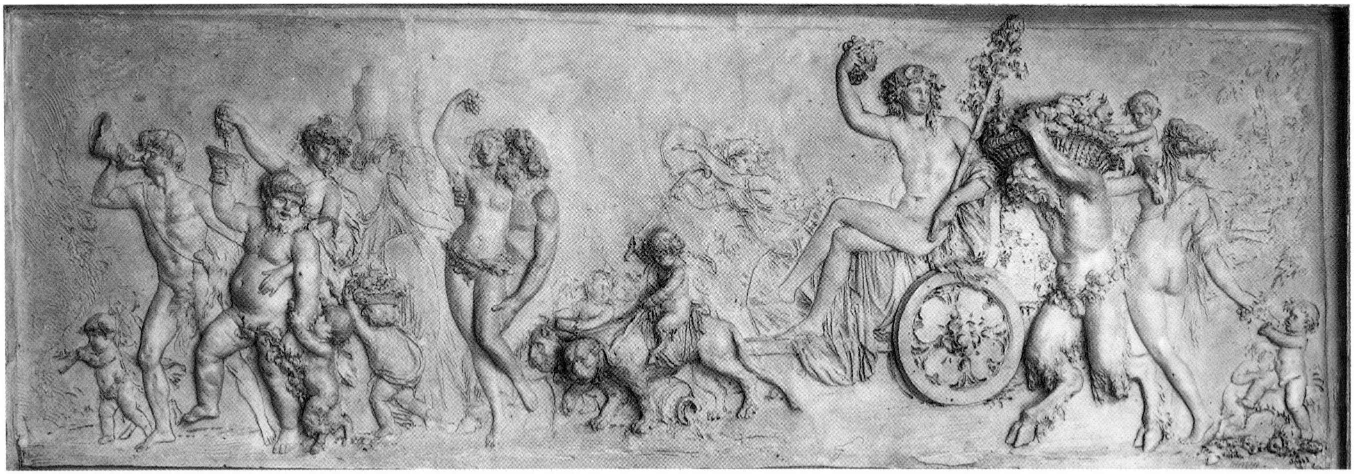

Fig. 5 Joseph-Charles Marin, *The Triumph of Bacchus*, c. 1790, terracotta, 37 × 109 cm, inscribed lower right: *Marin*
National Gallery of Canada, Ottawa

Marino) than to his earlier treatment of the theme.[19] The sanctity of kinship, the satisfaction that comes with secure knowledge of one's place in society and the rewards of a job well done — these are the inviolable values promoted in both pictures. These same values would continue to be reinforced in peasant genre painting throughout the next century, in the works of Millet, Breton, Clausen and a host of others. As Hayes has observed, Gainsborough's late landscapes and 'fancy pictures' thus stand on the threshold of a romantic sensibility: they look nostalgically to the traditional structures of a society already in flux and ignore the harsh realities of peasant labour.[20]

Traditionally, the Toronto *Harvest Wagon* and a slightly earlier canvas of the same size, *Rocky Wooded Upland Landscape* (1783, fig. 6)[21], have been considered a commissioned pair from their first owner the Prince of Wales who was, as is well known, a friend and patron of the artist.[22] According to Hayes, however, only the Munich landscape was a commission, and the Toronto *Harvest Wagon* a subsequent purchase. The pictures are referred to as princely commissions as early as 1789, in the posthumous exhibition and sale of Gainsborough's pictures organized by the artist's nephew and widow at Schomberg House in the spring of that year.[23] According to Waterhouse, they are the "two large Landskips" valued at £210 listed among thirteen works painted "for His Royal Highness, the Prince of Wales" billed cumulatively to him between 1781 and 1784,[24] and indeed, of the four

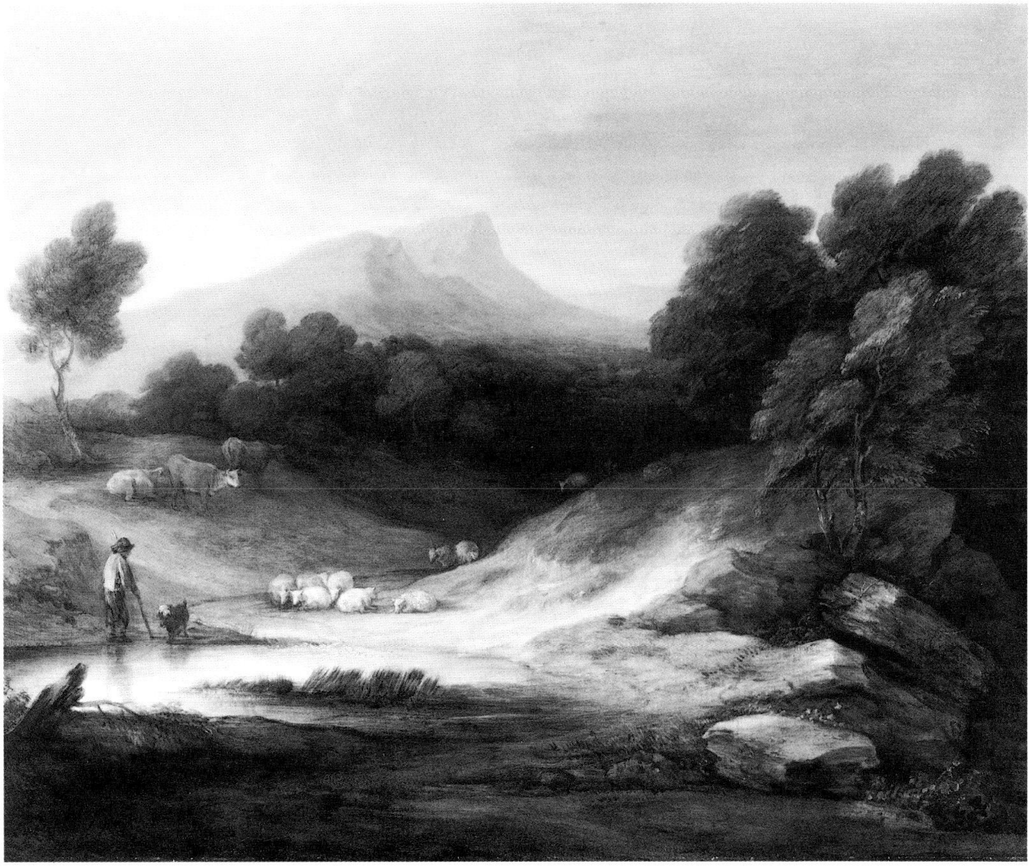

Fig. 6 Thomas Gainsborough, *Rocky Wooded Upland Landscape*, 1783, oil on canvas, 120 × 148.6 cm, signed bottom right: *T.G.* Bayerische Landesbank, on loan to the Neue Pinakothek, Munich

Gainsborough landscapes that the Prince owned during his lifetime, only two were acquired from the artist.[25] Beyond confirming the level of the Prince's patronage towards Gainsborough over a four-year period, this document is important insofar as it itemises both landscapes under one rubric (thereby at least implying a relationship between the two), and furthermore, states that they were executed as commissions by June 1784.[26]

For Hayes, the *terminus ante quem* for the dating of the Toronto *Harvest Wagon* is provided by its first published description, by Bate-Dudley in late January 1785: "Mr. Gainsborough's celebrated landscape consists of an evening scene; the principal object of it, a farm cart returning from a country market."[27] Hayes bases his dating of the picture to the winter of 1784 on this document. If Waterhouse's identification is correct, however, we must conclude that the work was completed at least six months earlier. If so, we are provided with a possible explanation as to how, by early 1785, it might already be described as "celebrated" in the chatty *Morning Herald.*

It is clearer, at any rate, that the Munich *Rocky Wooded Upland Landscape* was a princely commission. On 26 July 1784, Bate-Dudley writes: "this Picture is, we understand, painted for the Prince of Wales,"[28] and according to Hayes, this was the picture for which he was charged 100 guineas in 1784.[29] If we are to assume, as we must, that this is one of the "pair of Landskips" in the bill published by Waterhouse, we must also conclude that the Toronto *Harvest Wagon* is the other, and that the Prince had acquired them by the summer of 1784. According to Hayes, the Munich painting was first exhibited in 1784, while the Toronto *Harvest Wagon* was only first seen at the Schomberg sale in 1789. Might Bate-Dudley's 1785 reference to the picture's reputation allude then to the prestige it had accrued through ownership?

The putative role of the Prince of Wales in the creation of the Toronto painting is nonetheless difficult to establish with certainty. Again in *The Morning Herald*, Bate-Dudley writes on 3 April 1786, that "the Prince of Wales has purchased Mr. Gainsborough's beautiful picture of the peasants returning from market: the Prince's taste for the fine arts cannot be better illustrated, than in the choice he has made of the above picture."[30] Given the topical nature of this publication, it seems unlikely that no less than fifteen months (and more likely some two years) following its completion the source of the commission would merit announcement, and no mention is made of a sister picture. It remains logical to interpret the notice as signalling, as Hayes has concluded, a simple purchase of the painting from Gainsborough's studio many months following its execution.

As with many works he acquired, the Prince of Wales took possession of his *Harvest Wagon* and *Rocky Wooded Upland Landscape* only some years later. His debt to Mrs. Gainsborough was settled in 1793, and there is no subsequent record of the pictures until 1810, when they were sent by the Prince's command from Carlton House to Maria Fitzherbert on 20 July (see cat. 22).[31] Most interesting is a reference to the frames made specially for them by Wyatt, who is surely the London carver and gilder Edward Wyatt (1784–1840) who received commissions for numerous frames, door panels and gilding projects at Carlton House between 1807 and 1813.[32] We can thus speculate that the Prince had planned at some point to incorporate the pictures into one or another of his grand schemes for the enlargement and redecoration of Carlton House and that, as occurred regularly in the course of the four decades of that ill-fated undertaking, he changed his mind. The Prince took up residence at Carlton House late in 1783 and immediately commissioned work towards major transformations; his acquisition of the two landscapes as early as July 1784 and no later than April 1786 suggests that installation at Carlton House might have been their first intended purpose.[33]

The Prince of Wales secretly married Maria Fitzherbert on 15 December 1785.[34] Whether his acquisition of Gainsborough's two landscapes is also related in some way to this period in their long relationship (see fig. 7) cannot be ascertained. His later gift to her of the two pictures was at any rate one of several documented events in the Prince's life as a collector in 1810 that signal a time of particularly focused activity. He had collected pictures since he was in his twenties when, under the guidance of Richard Cosway (cat. 22), he favoured Italian 16th and 17th century works.[35] By around 1800 his interest had shifted to Dutch and Flemish art, culminating in the acquisition of

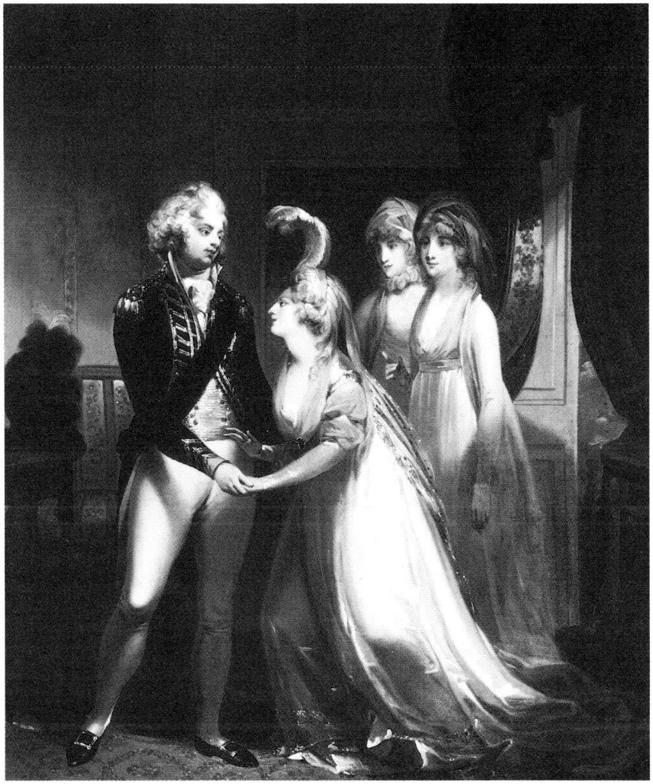

Fig. 7 Henry Singleton, *George IV and Mrs. Fitzherbert*, oil on canvas, 59.7 × 48.3 cm, Baltimore Museum of Art, Bequest of Elise Agnus Daingerfield

the Baring collection in 1814. He was a passionate supporter of contemporary British painting throughout his collecting career, attending the Royal Academy's annual dinners and lending works to the British Institution's exhibitions from its founding in 1805. Farington records that in 1810 he declared his wish to collect British art; since as we know, he had been doing so for some years, his remark should be seen in terms of renewed interest and emphasis.[36] That year he acquired a number of pictures from the collection of Walsh Porter, who had advised him on interior decorations at Carlton House from 1805 to 1809.[37] He acquired three portraits by Hoppner and presented one of them to his friend Lord Yarmouth.[38] Reynolds's two grand portraits of the Marquis of Granby and Count Lippe were given to the Prince by Lady Townsend the same year.[39]

Maria Fitzherbert bequeathed her Gainsborough landscapes to her son-in-law George Dawson Damer,[40] from whose collection they were auctioned in 1841, again as "painted expressedly for the Prince of Wales".[41] The pair was afterwards separated, and the Toronto *Harvest Wagon* passed through several hands in relative obscurity until it crossed the Atlantic in 1913 to enter the collection of Judge Elbert H. Gary (1846–1927), who with J. P. Morgan formed the industrial giant, the United States Steel Corporation. His collection, housed in a Fifth Avenue Renaissance-revival mansion in Manhattan, typified the taste of the American 'robber baron' heyday, and included French and English eighteenth-century painting, French furniture and Chinese porcelain. The sale of his collection in 1928 was the highlight of the New York auction season, not the least for the animated competition among Governor Alvan T. Fuller, Sir Joseph Duveen, Knoedler and Co. and Howard Young Galleries for *The Harvest Wagon*.[42] Ironically, the painting's princely connection had been forgotten during the intervening decades and no mention of its first owner is to be found in either the auction catalogue or the extensive press coverage of the sale and its record results. By this time Gainsborough's reputation was itself guarantee enough for the success of a first-rate example of his work in the burgeoning North American market.

The impact of Gainsborough's landscapes on English artists has been studied in depth by Hayes.[43] Francis Wheatley's *Harvest Wagon* of 1774 (cat. 15) is of particular interest in this context. Identified as a pastiche of the Barber *Harvest Wagon*,[44] it thus demonstrates Gainsborough's influence at an early stage. In addition, its similarities to the composition of the Toronto *Harvest Wagon* and especially of the *Wooded Landscape with Peasants, Country Carts, Faggot-gatherers and Barn*, also of c. 1784–5 (cat. 23) are unmistakable, and should be seen as evidence of a more complex and reciprocal relationship between Gainsborough and his contemporaries.

Copies of the Barber *Harvest Wagon* are known (fig. 8),[45] and two reduced replicas of the Toronto picture are recorded. One of these, whose quality precludes attribution to Gainsborough, is at Raveningham Hall, Norwich,[46] and the other was with Leggatt in 1952.[47] Interestingly, a repetition in the same format as the Leggatt picture exists of the Munich *Rocky Wooded Upland Landscape* (fig. 6), given to Gainsborough by Hayes.[48] Attributional issues notwithstanding, the existence of these two pictures might be taken as further evidence of the early pairing of the Toronto and Munich landscapes. Finally, a free, broadly sketched copy with the figures much rearranged, attributed by Hayes to Thomas Barker, is in the Toledo Museum of Art (cat. 25).

We need look no further than Constable's great *Haywain* for tangible evidence of that artist's touching acknowledgment of his debt to Gainsborough: "The landscape of Gainsborough is soothing, tender and affecting ... On looking at them, we find tears in our eyes, and know not what brings them."[49] Reynolds's posthumous tribute to his great rival, delivered to the students of the Royal Academy on 10 December 1788, was predictably more reserved, and while he allowed that "if ever this nation should produce genius sufficient to acquire to us the honourable distinction of an English School, the name of Gainsborough will be transmitted to posterity," he criticised Gainsborough's "want of precision and finishing" and cautioned his audience that "no apology can be made for this deficiency, in that style which this academy teaches, and which ought to be the object of your pursuit."[50] To be sure, Gainsborough

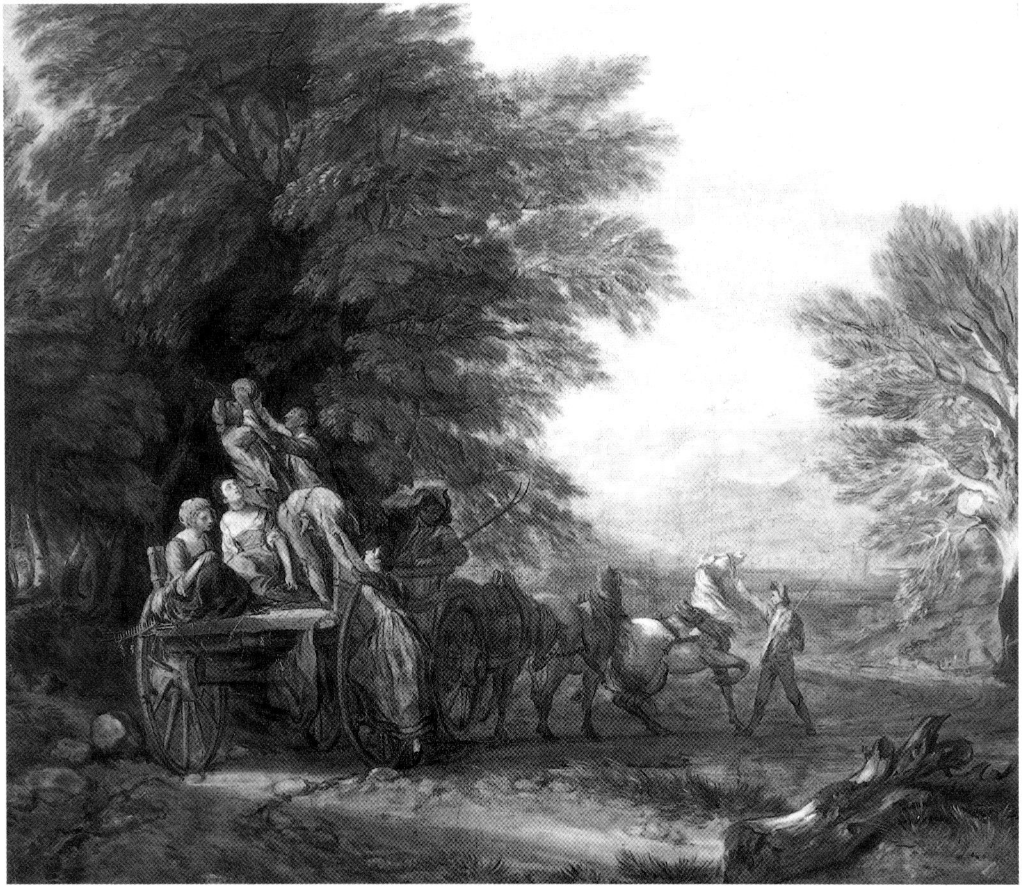

Fig. 8 After Gainsborough, *The Harvest Wagon*, (Barber version), oil on canvas, 81 × 96.5 cm, formerly New York, Metropolitan Museum of Art. Photo © 1979 Sotheby's Inc.

never aspired to the grand manner as interpreted in the history painting of Reynolds or West. But he raised the art of landscape to loftier heights through his assimilation of the lessons of Rubens and the French rococo. In paintings like the Barber and Toronto *Harvest Wagons*, Gainsborough reinterpreted these sources to create a new type of landscape painting that imbued his subject with a nobler voice than ever before in English painting. In introducing subtle narrative to these paintings, Gainsborough anticipated the peasant genre – with its moralising and anecdotal overtones – that would dominate much of English and French painting during the next century.

1 William Hazlitt, 'On Gainsborough's Pictures,' *The Champion*, 31 July 1814, reprinted in: *The Complete Works of William Hazlitt*, ed. P. P. Howe, XVIII, London and Toronto, 1933, p. 36.
2 In 1772 he described it in metaphors curiously relevant to the *Harvest Wagon* compositions that are the subject of this exhibition: "I hate ... being confined *in Harness* to follow the track, whilst others ride in the waggon, under cover, stretching their Legs in the straw at Ease, and gazing at Green Trees & Blue skies without half my *Taste*." (Woodall, *Letters*, no. 56, p. 115).
3 Hayes, nos. 95 and 107. Hayes, furthermore, documents only one example (no. 106) – in which authenticity is questionable – of Gainsborough painting a full-scale replica of a landscape.
4 Woodall, *Letters*, no. 79, p. 143, in reference to his two Academy submissions that year. Traditionally the Barber *Harvest Wagon* is counted as one of these, but the identification is thought uncertain by Hayes (Hayes, p. 430). See also p. 22, note 5 in this volume.
5 *The Morning Post*, 27 April 1778, quoted in John Hayes, 'Gainsborough and Rubens,' *Apollo*, LXXVIII, August 1963, note 20.
6 Horace Walpole, *Anecdotes of Painting in England*, II, Strawberry Hill, 1762, p. 81. The sentiment is echoed by Uvedale Price, for whom Rubens "in point of brilliancy, of extreme splendour of light, no pictures can stand in competition" (*An Essay on the Picturesque*, first publ. 1794, Edinburgh & London, 1842, p. 116).
7 Wolfgang Adler, *Corpus Rubenianum Ludwig Burchard; Part XVIII: Landscapes and Hunting Scenes. I: Landscapes*, London, 1982, no. 19, where the Harcourt picture is listed as a copy.
8 C. G. Voorhelm Schneevoogt, *Catalogue des estampes gravées d'après P. P. Rubens*, Haarlem, 1873, p. 233, no. 53, 5.
9 Hayes, p. 145 and no. 157.
10 Hayes, 1963, p. 94.
11 Diane Carole Bliss, 'Thomas Gainsborough 1727–1788' in: Providence (RI), Brown University, Bell Gallery, *Rubenism*, 1975, pp. 201–205.
12 *The Diary of Joseph Farington*, IV, ed. K. Garlick and A. Macintyre, New Haven and London, 1979, p. 1149 (30 January 1799). Gainsborough owned three portraits ascribed to Van Dyck and made copies of at least four more. See [Tancred Borenius], 'Gainsborough's Collection of Pictures,' *Burlington Magazine*, LXXXIV, May 1944, pp. 108–110, nos 6, 14, 18 and 57, 65, 73, 92.
13 Hayes, no. 160.
14 Hayes, p. 532.
15 Hayes, 1963, note 16.
16 Ellis K. Waterhouse, 'Gainsborough's "Fancy Pictures,"' *Burlington Magazine*, LXXXVIII, June 1946, p. 134.
17 Marcia Pointon, 'Gainsborough and the Landscape of Retirement,' *Art History*, II-4, December 1979, pp. 441–455. See also by the same author *Milton & English Art*, Toronto, 1970, and Maynard Mack, *The Garden and the City; Retirement and Politics in the Later Poetry of Pope 1731–1743*, Oxford, 1969. For a dissenting view see Hayes, p. 150.
18 Woodall, *Letters*, no. 56, p. 115.
19 Hayes, no. 123.
20 Hayes, p. 151.
21 Hayes, no. 146.
22 For a concise survey of their relationship, see Oliver Millar, *The Later Georgian Pictures in the Collection of Her Majesty the Queen*, London, 1969, I, pp. xxvi-xxvii.
23 The catalogue for this sale is reprinted in [Borenius], 1944, pp. 107-110. Nos. 74 and 75 are described as "A Landscape, with a Wagon and Figures returning from Market" and "Ditto, its Companion[;] The Above two Pictures are his Royal Highness the Prince of Wales's, for whom they were painted, but have not yet been sent home" (p. 109). The two canvasses were not among the items for sale, but as their owner had not taken possession (Gainsborough's widow received payment for them only in 1793, at the settlement of the Prince's debts), their inclusion was certainly intended to augment the prestige of the event, and was interpreted as such in the press on opening day: "The Prince of Wales visits Gainsborough's Pictures previous to the sale. His Royal Highness possesses already two landscapes from that charming artist, but as these fine Portraits of Nature in her rustic garb will not hereafter be attainable, it is supposed, that the taste of his Royal Highness will not on the present occasion pass by." (*The Morning Post*, 30 March 1789, p. 3). I am grateful to David A. Brenneman, Assistant Curator of Paintings, Yale Center for British Art, for this reference. An erroneous account is later given in *Notes and Queries*, 25 November 1871, p. 434: "[the Prince] sought to set the tide of fashion towards purchasing the unsold pictures at

Schomberg House ... and gave 2000 guineas [sic] for two landscapes, which he presented to Nesbitt's neighbour, Mrs. Fitzherbert."

24 Ellis K. Waterhouse, 'A Gainsborough Bill for the Prince of Wales,' *Burlington Magazine*, LXXXVIII, November 1946, p. 276. According to Millar, 1969, p. 35, the bill was probably drawn up by Mrs. Gainsborough following her husband's death (and must therefore date between 1788 and 1793, when the debt was finally settled).

25 The other two were acquired from Margaret Gainsborough after 1799 and in 1797 at the Mrs. Gainsborough sale (Hayes, nos. 116 and 160).

26 The dates in this document clearly refer to acquisition by the Prince, not the dates of execution; for example, the "full-length of Mrs. Robinson" valued at £105, now in the Wallace Collection, is also listed under June 1784, but was painted in 1781, and the "Head of Mrs. Elliot" under the same date had been exhibited in 1782.

27 *The Morning Herald*, 27 January 1785, p. 2.

28 *The Morning Herald*, 26 July 1784.

29 Hayes, p. 181.

30 *The Morning Herald*, 3 April 1786, p. 2.

31 Millar, 1969, p. 35, citing f.68 of Benjamin Jutsham's day-book, "1806 An Account of Furniture &c Received and Deliver'd ... on Account of His Royal Highness The Prince of Wales at Carlton House" which records the despatch of goods between 1807 and 1830.

32 Geoffrey Beard and Christopher Gilbert, *Dictionary of English Furniture Makers 1660–1840*, Leeds, 1986, pp. 1009–1010. See also exh. cat., London, Buckingham Palace, The Queen's Gallery, *Carlton House; The Past Glories of George IV's Palace*, 1991–1992, p. 31. The frames would probably have been in a massive and ornate neoclassical style favoured at Carlton House. These frames are sadly no longer with the pictures; the Toronto *Harvest Wagon* is now framed in a magnificient (if inappropriate) French eighteenth-century style frame typical of those commissioned during the late 19th and early 20th centuries from the Paris framer Bourdier by Duveen (who owned the picture in 1928; see below, note 42). Duveen reserved this frame style for his most important pictures, the best known being Rembrandt's *Aristotle contemplating the Bust of Homer* (Metropolitan Museum, New York), which he also acquired in 1928. I am grateful to Paul Mitchell for this information.

33 Inventory records for Carlton House list over 250 pictures in store; see *Carlton House*, 1991–2, p. 26.

34 The marriage was declared illegal and in 1795 he was married to Princess Caroline of Brunswick.

35 Stephen Lloyd, 'Forming the Taste of a Prince; Richard Cosway and George IV's Early Collecting,' *Apollo*, CXXXVIII, September 1993, p. 192.

36 *The Diary of Joseph Farington*, X, ed. K. Cave, New Haven and London, 1982, p. 3691: "[West] told me He had been with the Prince of Wales who seemed much disposed to make a Collection of the works of British Artists"; see also *Carlton House*, 1991–2, p. 41.

37 Sold London, Christie's, 14 April 1810.

38 Painted c. 1792-6; now Wallace Collection, London.

39 *Carlton House*, 1991–2, p. 26.

40 By codicil; reproduced in Shane Leslie, *Mrs. Fitzherbert; A Life Chiefly from Unpublished Sources*, New York, 1939, p. 385–6. His wife was Fitzherbert's adopted daughter (and according to various sources either her niece or illegitimate child).

41 London, Christie's, 27 March 1841, lots 141–2 (bought in).

42 *New York Times*, 21 April 1928. The picture was knocked down to Duveen for $360,000, a record for any painting sold in America until 1961 (Thomas E. Norton, *100 Years of Collecting in America; The Story of Sotheby Parke Bernet*, New York, 1984, p. 106). See also Esther Singleton, *Old World Masters in New World Collections*, New York, 1929, pp. 389–392, where the hammer price is erroneously recorded as $875,000 and the picture's history is conflated with that of the Barber *Harvest Wagon*.

43 Hayes, pp. 237–298.

44 Hayes, p. 24.

45 A grisaille oil (fig. 8) was at the Metropolitan Museum, New York (sold New York, Sotheby Parke Bernet, 16 March 1979, lot 89) and a chalk drawing signed and dated 1771 (fig. 1) was acquired by Dr. Sigmund Samuel, Toronto from London, Sotheby's 27 July 1960, no. 56. The current locations of these works are unknown.

46 Oil on canvas, 33.3 × 43.5 cm; photograph in the Witt Library, Courtauld Institute.

47 Oil on canvas, 71.7 × 92 cm; reproduced in *Burlington Magazine*, XCIV, February 1952, p. i.

48 Hayes, no. 147.

49 From Constable's Fourth Lecture at the Royal Institution, 16 June 1836; publ. in C. R. Leslie, *Life and Letters of John Constable, R.A.*, London, 1896, p. 397.

50 Sir Joshua Reynolds, *Discourses on Art*, ed. R. Wark, San Marino, 1959, pp. 260–1.

CATALOGUE

Unless otherwise stated, all works are by Gainsborough.
Some works are exhibited at Birmingham or Toronto only.
This is indicated throughout the catalogue by
the abbreviations [B] or [T] respectively.

1
The Harvest Wagon [Plate I, p. 8]
1767
Oil on canvas, 120.5 × 144.7 cm.
The Trustees of the Barber Institute of Fine Arts,
The University of Birmingham
(Hayes, no. 88)

The landscape background of this, the first of Gainsborough's versions of the harvest wagon theme, was traditionally inspired by Shockerwick Park, Bathford, the home of Gainsborough's "warm and personal friend",[1] the wealthy carrier, Walter Wiltshire. No drawings of Shockerwick have been identified, however, and according to one early account the scene was based on an incident which Gainsborough had witnessed near Chippenham.[2] Attempts to identify a precise location remain unsuccessful, since the distance and hills are very freely painted and the church in the right background is vague.[3]

The figure composition is the most elaborate ever attempted by the artist and is subtly derived from his knowledge of Rubens's *Descent from the Cross* (see cat. 8) which he knew from the modello (fig. 3) then at Corsham Court, near Bath, and, more directly, through the engraving by Lucas Vorsterman (cat. 9). The influence of Rubens is also clearly discernible in the energetic handling of the grey horse and the clouds. Compositionally, however, the work owes much to Claude, especially the *repoussoir* groups of trees, the winding roadway and the focus on a small but crucial silhouetted building. Gainsborough's knowledge and love of Watteau and French rococo painting is reflected in the feathery foliage of the trees. Yet despite the structural and stylistic complexity of the work, X-rays show that Gainsborough made no appreciable alterations to the composition during the course of its execution.[4]

Gainsborough used models for at least some of the figures – most notably that of the girl being pulled up into the wagon, whose features are based on those of his younger daughter, Margaret (cat. 12). It is very likely that the girl looking up is based on her older sister, Mary (fig. 4). The stiffness of her neck and right arm suggest that a lay figure was employed for the body.

The leading horse is believed to have been a favourite of Gainsborough's, which he rode when at Shockerwick, and which was given to him by Wiltshire, when the artist left Bath in 1774. Together with its companions, it is one of a kind whose qualities of roughness appealed to Gainsborough's picturesque susceptibilities (cf. cat. 42). In the present context, however, its key position gives it a monumental character, more reminiscent of ancient sculpture, and its conjunction with the drover brings to mind the famous group of *The Horse Tamers* as a prototype.

The Harvest Wagon was exhibited at the Society of Artists in London in 1767. When Gainsborough moved from Bath to London he presented it to Wiltshire in return for the horse.

A reduced grisaille copy was formerly in the Metropolitan Museum, New York (fig. 8).[5]

For a fuller account of the picture, see the first introductory essay to the catalogue (pp. 10–23). For provenance, exhibitions and bibliography, see pp. 68–70.

1 Edward and William Finden, *The Royal Gallery of British Art*, London, 1843, unpaginated text with the engraving of *The Harvest Wagon* (cat. 40).
2 Ibid.
3 The painting was damaged by a fire extinguisher, and a vertical band of repaired damage passes through the building, obscuring its outline. It was, however, clearly understood as a church by the nineteenth-century engravers, Finden and Josey (cats. 40 and 41). A similarity to the tower of St Gregory's, Sudbury, has been noted, but if a specific reference is intended it is more likely to be a church in the vicinity of Bath, perhaps All Saints, Weston.
4 X-rays of the entire picture were taken at the Louvre in 1981 on the occasion of its exhibition at the Grand Palais, Paris.
5 Previously lot 37 in the S. G. Holland sale, Christie's, 25 June 1908.

2

The Harvest Wagon [Plate II, p. 9]
1784/5
Oil on canvas, 121.9 × 149.9 cm.
Signed with initials on rock below foreground sheep: *T.G.*
Art Gallery of Ontario, Toronto, Gift of Mr. and Mrs. Frank P. Wood, 1941
(Hayes, no. 157)

Considered together, Gainsborough's two versions of *The Harvest Wagon* can reasonably be seen as the artist's most compelling achievement in landscape painting. In them, Gainsborough forged a pictorial language in which genre elements are brought forward to the picture plane and wedded seamlessly to their landscape setting. In so doing, he contributed to the creation of a new genre that would culminate spectacularly in his own last pictures, such as *The Market Cart* of 1786/7 (cat. 24), and herald, further, the peasant genre painting that dominated much English and French painting of the next generation.

The existence of these two pictures, so alike in subject-matter but separated in date by almost twenty years, is unique in Gainsborough's production, and suggests the subject's importance for the artist. We know that Gainsborough continued to consider the Barber picture among his best landscapes well into the 1770s, and his reprise of the theme towards the end of his career is additional testimony to the status of the first version for Gainsborough and his contemporaries. Certainly, the acquisition of the Toronto landscape by the Prince of Wales, possibly by commission but certainly within two years of its execution, should be seen as confirmation of the regard in which the composition was held.

For us, the two *Harvest Wagons* provide an unusual opportunity to examine the progress of Gainsborough's stylistic evolution from mid to late career through the 'constant' of picture size and subject-matter. In the Barber version, the influence of the artist's French contemporaries that pervaded his work in the 1760s is evident in the delicate brushwork, the clear, warm palette and elegant deportment of figures. Yet the source for the disposition of figures in the cart is Rubens, whose *Descent from the Cross* demonstrably determined its unusual pyramidal structure (see cats. 8 and 9). An explicit debt to Rubens is similarly present in the Toronto version, where the tilted cart and rocky landscape extrusion appear to derive from the composition of the Flemish artist's *Mired Cart* (cat. 16). More importantly, however, Rubens's influence has here evolved from formal citation to stylistic assimilation: the dark, dramatic palette dominated by brown and blue tones, the robust brushwork and the theatrical spotlighting of the figures in the wagon testify to the dominant influence of Rubens on Gainsborough's late work and reflect the growing regard for Rubens's landscapes among English collectors and critics during the second half of the eighteenth century (see cats. 26 and 27).

As is the case with much of Gainsborough's painted work, no drawings are directly related to the composition of the Toronto *Harvest Wagon*; the numerous works on paper that include wagons and carts are evidence not of preparation for the painting, but of the compelling interest the subject held for the artist throughout his career. Recent X-ray examination of the painting shows that Gainsborough made no changes to it during the course of its execution.

An untraced smaller version of the Toronto *Harvest Wagon*, of uncertain attribution, appeared with Leggatt in 1952, there identified as from Sir George Beaumont's collection. This picture may be the one that appears on the left wall in William Frederick Witherington's painting identified in the Royal Academy exhibition of 1824 as *A Modern Picture Gallery* and traditionally identified as Sir John Fleming Leicester's collection (now Wimpole Hall).[1]

A drawing attributed to Thomas Rowlandson at Christchurch Mansion, Ipswich and a painting by Thomas Barker (cat. 25) both derive from the Toronto composition, and attest further to its impact on the subsequent generation.

For a fuller account of this picture, see the second introductory essay to the catalogue (pp. 24-32). For provenance, exhibitions and bibliography, see pp. 70–72.

1 According to Alastair Laing, only some of the pictures (all British) reproduced in Witherington's painting can be identified as Leicester's (letter to the authors 1 September 1994). See also London, Dulwich Picture Gallery, *Palaces of Art; Art Galleries in Great Britain 1790–1990*, exh. cat. 1991, no. A20.

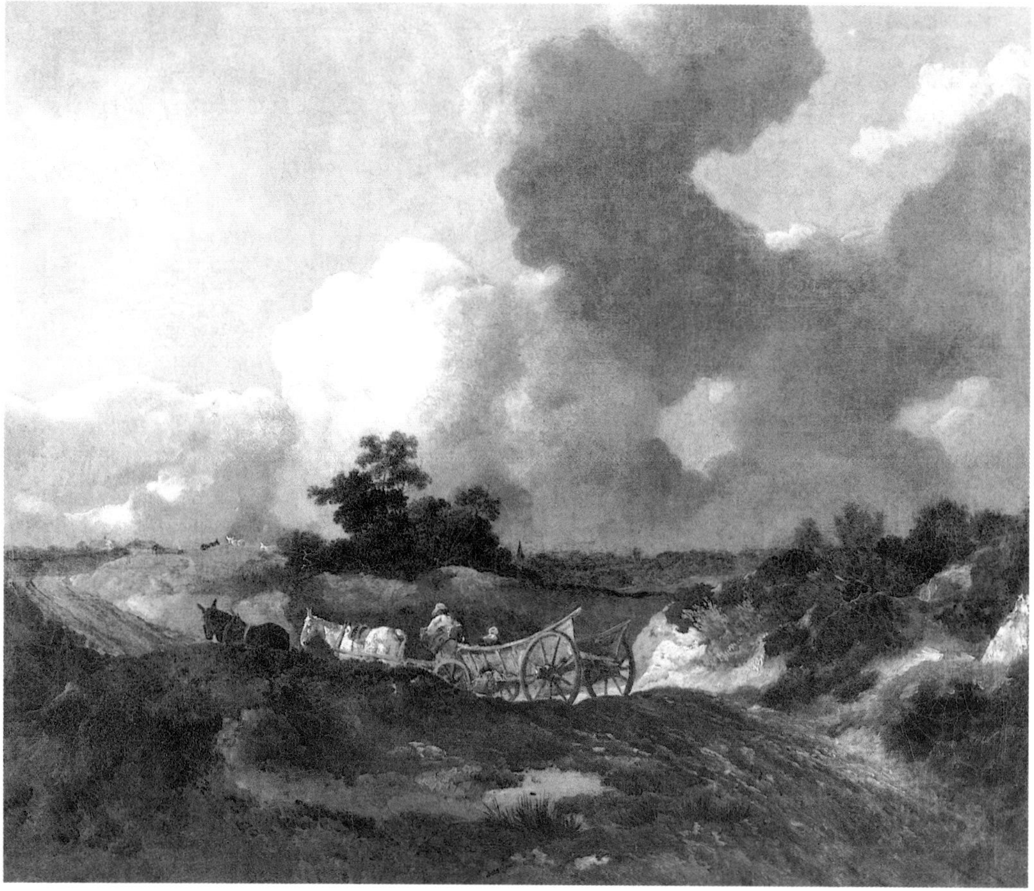

Cat. 3 Gainsborough, *Landscape with Country Wagon*, Rothschild Trust, Canada Inc.

3
Landscape with Country Wagon
c. 1746–7
Oil on canvas, 49.3 × 60.5 cm.
Rothschild Trust, Canada Inc.
(Hayes, no. 12)

One of Gainsborough's earliest paintings, executed when he was working in London and greatly influenced by Dutch masters. This is particularly noticeable in the treatment of the dark grey clouds within the large expanse of sky and the dune-like aspect of the landscape itself. Set within a terrain which recalls the Suffolk Gainsborough knew so well, an empty four-wheeled farm wagon, very much like that featured in both the Barber and Toronto *Harvest Wagons* and similarly seen from behind, is depicted midway along a winding track on its journey towards the horizon. Landscape and sky are both reminiscent of Dutch seventeenth-century landscapes, such as those by Jan Wijnants. The undulating track leads the eye towards a horizon which is itself irregular in silhouette and punctuated at intervals with donkeys, trees and a church. As a device for uniting the different planes of the landscape this is only partly successful. In the centre foreground the motif of pond with rushes in silhouette is adumbrated – one that was later used in other works by the artist, including the Barber *Harvest Wagon.* Even at this early stage, Gainsborough's instinctive sense of colour and tonal composition is apparent, notably in the yellowy greens, browns, greys and impastoed cream of the bank in the right middleground.

This is the first landscape by Gainsborough in which a country wagon makes an appearance as the principal subject (an earlier and smaller picture shows a cart, but not so prominently[1]). The wagon is almost empty, with just a tied sack visible behind the highlighted driver, and in this respect as well as in its orientation, prefigures a number of later landscapes including *Wooded Landscape with Country Wagon, Milkmaid and Drover* (cat. 6). As in that painting and the Barber *Harvest Wagon*, wisps of hay or straw are visible in the back of the wagon.

Landscape with Country Wagon was one of a pair of pictures whose first recorded owner was the Rev. Thomas Rackett (1757–1841), an amateur draughtsman, noted antiquary and executor of Gainsborough's friend, the actor, David Garrick. At least one copy (Private Collection, U.S.A.) was made by Julius Caesar Ibbetson[2] (1759–1817) and the composition was engraved in mezzotint by William Giller (c.1805–after 1868).

1 Gardner collection, Wickhambrook; Hayes, no. 7.
2 Hayes, p. 243 and pl. 278.

4
The Artist in his Early Thirties [Frontispiece]
c. 1758–9
Oil on canvas, 76.2 × 63.4 cm.
The National Portrait Gallery, London
(Waterhouse, no. 291)
[B]

Gainsborough depicts himself at the threshold of his career in Bath. Indeed the formality of the pose, and costume, with hand in waistcoat and hat visible under elbow, together with the carefully directed highlighting of the face suggest that the painting was intended as a demonstration of his abilities to prospective clients. It may thus have been displayed in the Pump Room, as was the custom in Bath for newly-arrived artists. Its technique is forward-looking in its broadness, and this is particularly evident in the handling of the leaves which frame his head.

Other single painted self-portraits of quarter-length format show Gainsborough in his twenties (1754, unfinished, Marquis of Cholmondeley) and in his sixties (c. 1787, Royal Academy, London).[1] Two other representations of him during his sojourn at Bath are known. One, attributed to William Hoare, Gainsborough's only serious rival as a portraitist in the city, shows him at the age of about forty (mid-1760s, Santa Barbara Museum of Art, California). The other, by Johann Zoffany, shows him a little older (c. 1771–2, Tate Gallery, London).

The two major constituents of Gainsborough's art, portraiture and landscape, are united in the present example, with portraiture taking physical precedence. The background foliage is subtly used, however, to suggest a laurel wreath of victory. Tension between the genres became particularly stressful to Gainsborough in the late 1760s, at the time when the *Harvest Wagon* was being painted. In 1772 he wrote to his friend, William Jackson, "I'm sick of Portraits and wish very much to take my Viol da Gamba and walk off to some sweet Village, when I can paint Landskips and enjoy the fag End of Life in quietness and ease".[2]

1 Waterhouse, nos. 290 and 292 respectively. He also appears, aged about 20, with a woman who is almost certainly his wife, in the double portrait in the Louvre, Waterhouse no. 752; and aged about 25, with wife and daughter, in the group portrait now in the National Gallery, London, but formerly in the Cholmondeley collection, Waterhouse, no. 296.
2 Letter to William Jackson, 4 June 1772: Woodall, *Letters*, no. 56, p. 115.

5

Margaret Gainsborough as a Gleaner

c. 1758–9

Oil on canvas, 73.7 × 63.5 cm.

The Visitors of the Ashmolean Museum, Oxford

(Waterhouse, no. 283)

Gainsborough's younger daughter, Margaret (1751–1820) is shown at the age of about seven, in the garb of a peasant girl. She was the younger of his two surviving children ("Molly and the Capt." as he sometimes called them). Her older sister, Mary, was born in 1750.[1] Almost a decade before the exhibition of the Barber *Harvest Wagon*, therefore, a connection was established in Gainsborough's mind between his daughters and the harvest process. In this respect the present picture looks forward to the later portrait of the same sitter (cat. 12), close in date to *The Harvest Wagon*, from which it is clear that the girl being pulled up into the wagon is indeed Margaret. *Margaret Gainsborough as a Gleaner*, however, makes a subtle contrast with *The Harvest Wagon* itself, where the girls are shown in fine costumes and having little to do with any actual harvesting or other agricultural process.

The condition of the right side of the picture, which was formerly torn at the edge, lends credence to the view that it was once part of a double portrait of the Gainsborough sisters. It was probably completed in its present form after cutting down in the nineteenth century, at which point the stems of the wheat were probably repainted. Documentary evidence of its original appearance is provided by a report in 1824 of a painting which "... represents portraits of his two daughters, in the garb of peasant girls, on the confines of a corn-field, dividing their gleanings. They appear to be of the age of about eight and nine, and are the size of life ... unfortunately [it is] left in part unfinished".[2] The artist portrayed the sisters together on five other occasions, of which the most contemporary example is *The Artist's Daughters teasing a Cat* (c.1758–9, National Gallery, London), also unfinished.[3]

The style of this painting accords with a date in the late 1750s, and it is executed in sweeping, fluent brush-strokes with grey-brown underpainting visible in areas such as the arms and neck. The cloudy blue grey sky is punctuated with brown, orange and pink highlights which, together with areas of grey, pink, purple and white on the child's chest and neck, suggest the influence of Rubens. The sitter's wistful and appealing expression and ragged clothing prefigure the 'fancy pictures' of peasant children which were to become a speciality of Gainsborough in the 1780s but also look forward to the Toronto *Harvest Wagon* which includes children in the figure group. Margaret Gainsborough's physiognomy may further betoken the eccentricity which characterised her behaviour in later life.

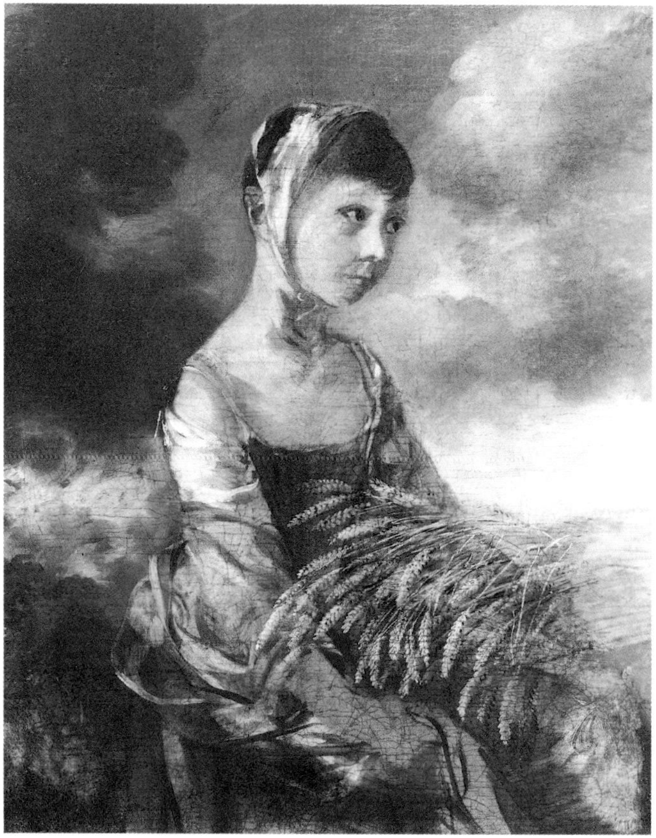

Cat. 5 Gainsborough,
Margaret Gainsborough as a Gleaner
The Ashmolean Museum, Oxford

1 Mary Gainsborough was baptised on 3 February 1750 and Margaret on 22 August 1751. See D. Tyler, 'The Gainsborough Family: Births, Marriages and Deaths Re-examined',

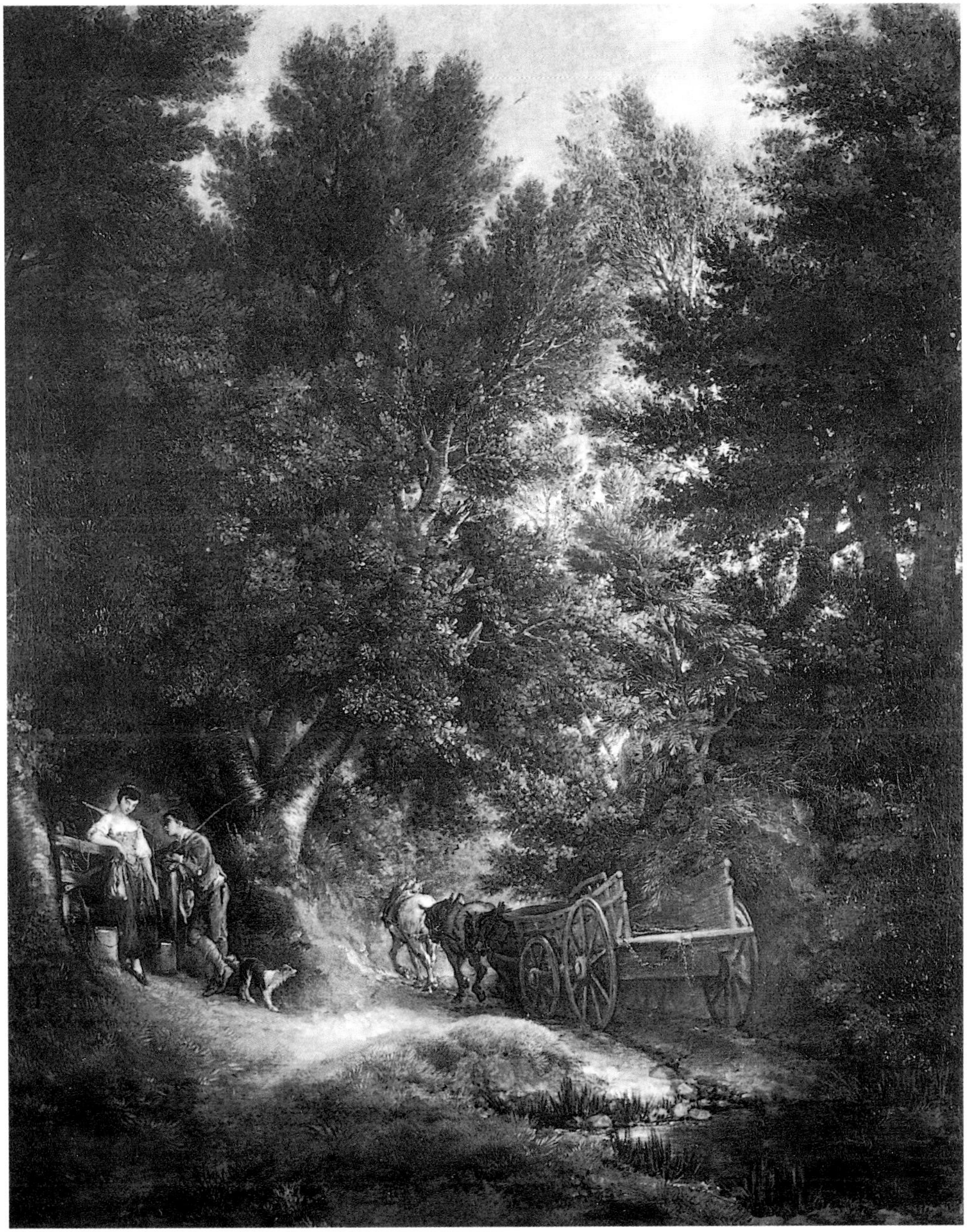

Cat. 6 Gainsborough,
Wooded Landscape with Country Wagon, Milkmaid and Drover,
Private Collection,
United Kingdom

Gainsborough's House Review, 1992/93, p. 42. For further information on Gainsborough's family, see Hugh Belsey, *Gainsborough's Family*, exh. cat., Gainsborough's House Society, Sudbury, 1988.
2 W.H. Pyne in the *Somerset House Gazette*, 7 August 1824, p. 272.
3 Others of the 1750s are *The Painter's Daughters chasing a Butterfly* (c. 1756, National Gallery, London; Waterhouse, no. 285) and *The Painter's Daughters* (c. 1758–9, Victoria and Albert Museum, London; Waterhouse, no. 284). The remaining portraits are *Mary and Margaret Gainsborough* (c.1763–4, Worcester Art Museum, Mass.; Waterhouse, no. 287) and *The Painter's Daughters* (early 1770s, Private Collection; Waterhouse, no. 288).

6

Wooded Landscape with Country Wagon, Milkmaid and Drover

1766
Oil on canvas, 144.8 × 119.4 cm.
Private Collection, United Kingdom
(Hayes, no. 87)

This was the second landscape which Gainsborough exhibited at the Society of Artists (the first was very probably the *Wooded Landscape with Horseman and Flock of Sheep*, now in the Worcester Art Museum, Mass.).[1] Painted just before the Barber *Harvest Wagon*, on two canvases joined together, it is the last large-scale landscape in Gainsborough's Dutch manner, which had dominated his early work. During the early 1760s, he was searching for an authentic grand style in landscape, with which to appeal to Bath collectors and challenge the supremacy of the classical masters of the seventeenth century, notably Claude and Gaspard Dughet. Here the solemn tonality and technical handling of the massed trees, which deny any distant vista to the viewer, are strongly reminiscent of the forest scenery of Hobbema and Jacob van Ruisdael. This is in marked contrast to the French-inspired sketchier effect of the foliage in *The Harvest Wagon*.

The motif of a four-wheeled box-wagon drawn by three horses, with a grey leader is adumbrated in this picture, which also shares with *The Harvest Wagon* the feature of a shallow pond at the lower right. To the left the milkmaid has something of the appearance of Gainsborough's daughter, Margaret (cats. 5 and 12). Rustic lovers frequently appear in earlier and later works, such as *Rocky Wooded Landscape with Rustic Lovers* (cat. 14), where the leaning, cross-legged pose of the youth is also used again. In the present case, despite their torn and ragged clothing, the milkmaid and her rustic beau are transformed into a romantic idyll, emphasised by powerful cross-lighting from the right. The dramatic contrast between areas of light and shadow very probably originated in Gainsborough's practice of painting landscapes by candlelight, which, according to his friend, the miniaturist, Ozias Humphrey, he adopted during this period.[2]

When this painting was exhibited at the Society of Artists in 1766 Horace Walpole referred to the couple memorably as a "milkmaid and clown".[3] Another, anonymous reviewer of that exhibition remarked: "In this picture there is much to be commended, the figures are in a fine taste, the cart-horses and fore-ground are extremely fine and well painted, but the trees are too blue and hard".[4] The bluey-greenness of the trees may well reflect Gainsborough's continuing interest in the style of Dutch artists such as Wijnants or the use of such colours by French contemporaries, notably Boucher.

Wooded Landscape with Country Wagon, Milkmaid and Drover was bought in 1766 by Sir William St Quintin, one of the artist's earliest patrons and a close friend during his Bath years. His account book for that year (now missing) shows that he paid £43-11s-6d for it. This price may be compared with Gainsborough's fees of 40 guineas for a half-length portrait and 60 guineas for a full-length at that time.

1 Hayes, no. 80.
2 Hayes, p. 98.
3 A. Graves, *Society of Artists of Great Britain*, London, 1907, p. 98.
4 Anon., *A Critical Review of the Pictures*, London, 1766, p. 6.

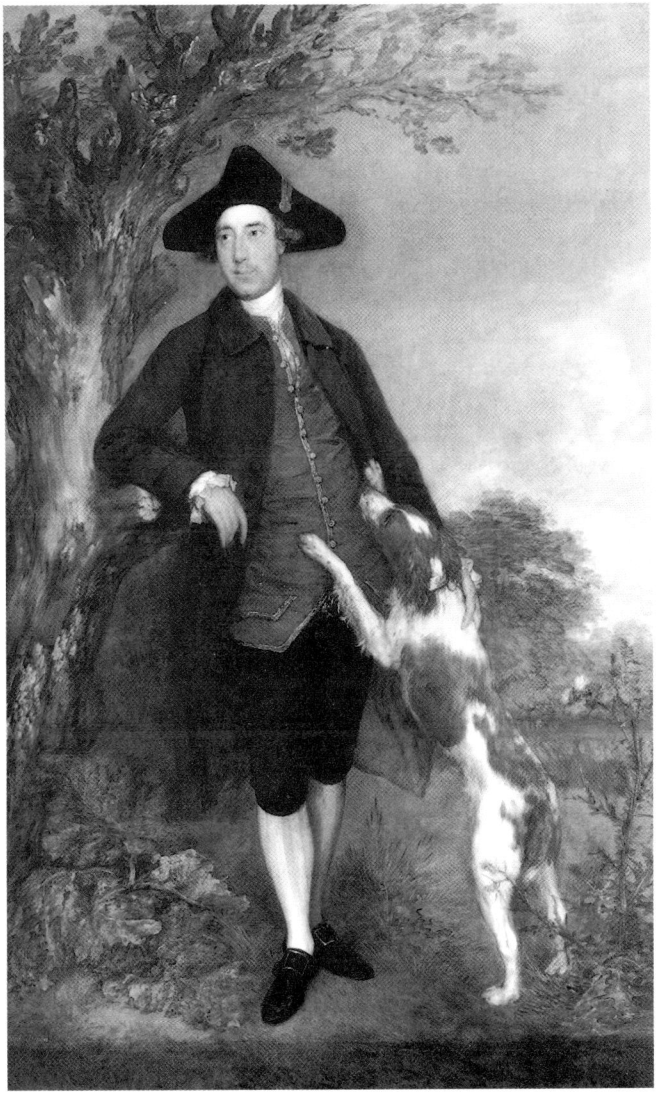

Cat. 7 Gainsborough, *George Venables Vernon, 2nd Lord Vernon*
Southampton City Art Gallery

7
George Venables Vernon, 2nd Lord Vernon
1767
Oil on canvas, 246.3 × 150.4 cm.
Southampton City Art Gallery
(Waterhouse, no. 693)
[B]

This is one of three impressive full-length portraits which Gainsborough sent to the Society of Artists in 1767, the same year as the Barber *Harvest Wagon*. The other two were *John, 4th Duke of Argyll*[1] and *Henrietta, Countess Grosvenor*.[2] Their dimensions symbolise the enforced predominance of portraiture in the artist's oeuvre at this time – *Lord Vernon* is twice the size of the *Harvest Wagon*.

George, 2nd Baron Vernon, was born in 1735 and died in 1813. He was a Whig M.P. from 1757, and at the time when this portrait was painted he represented the Sussex seat of Bramber, near Worthing. In 1780 he succeeded to his father's title and the fortuitously named family seat of Sudbury Hall, Derbyshire.

In its lightness of tone and freshness of handling the portrait announces Gainsborough's departure from his Dutch inspired manner and is directly comparable with the Barber *Harvest Wagon*. It is instructive to compare the particularised handling of the foreground burdock and thistle, and the fluent but sketchy tree-trunk with those of the Barber *Harvest Wagon*, whose compositional devices of large framing tree and strong diagonal axis are also present in the portrait. *Lord Vernon* is the first of Gainsborough's portraits to show the influence of Rubens in its landscape background.[3] This is especially marked in the thickly impastoed yellow passages of the sky by the tree at the far right.

The elegant nonchalance and dreamy expression of Lord Vernon, however, and the attentive spaniel owe much to the example of Van Dyck, for whom Gainsborough's enthusiasm during the 1760s is well known.[4] In this he was not only responding to aristocratic expectations, but also following the leading commentators of the day, notably Reynolds and Horace Walpole. Seven copies after Van Dyck are listed in the 1789 sale catalogue of the contents of his studio[5] and his admiration for the artist is embodied in the famous letter of 1768 to David Garrick, urging him to visit the Duke of Montagu's so as to see "the 4 Vandykes whole length in his Grace's dressing-room".[6] He also owned three portraits by or attributed to Van Dyck[7], and thirty-five prints after the artist.

Gainsborough's fifteen years in Bath were largely devoted to portraiture. It was there that he first encountered the class of fashionable sitter represented by Lord Vernon. By the mid-1760s he was well established, with no rival apart from William Hoare.

1 Scottish National Portrait Gallery, Edinburgh; Waterhouse, no. 19.
2 Private Collection, United Kingdom; Waterhouse, no. 332.
3 The sitter was, co-incidentally, related through Martha, his step-mother, to Simon, 1st Earl Harcourt, of Nuneham Courtenay, owner of a copy of Rubens's *Mired Cart* (cat. 16).
4 See D. Cherry and J. Harris, 'Eighteenth-Century Portraiture and the Seventeenth-Century Past: Gainsborough and Van Dyck,' *Art History*, vol. 5, no. 3, Sept. 1982, pp. 287–309. Dogs play significant roles in several portraits of English sitters by Van Dyck, eg. *James Stuart, Duke of Lennox and Richmond*, Metropolitan Museum, New York, 89.15.16, formerly Methuen Collection, Corsham.
5 [Tancred Borenius], 'Gainsborough's Collection of Pictures,' *Burlington Magazine*, LXXXIV, 1944, pp. 108–9, nos. 17, 41, 57, 65, 73, 92, 94.
6 Woodall, *Letters*, no. 27, p. 67.
7 [Borenius, 1944], pp. 108–9, nos. 6, 14, 18.

8
The Descent from the Cross (after Rubens)
[Plate III, p. 11]
Early to mid 1760s
Oil on canvas, 121.9 × 97.9 cm.
Private Collection, United Kingdom, on loan to the Ashmolean Museum, Oxford
(Waterhouse, no. 1027)

9
Lucas Vorsterman I (Flemish, 1595–1675)
The Descent from the Cross (after Rubens)
1620
Engraving, 585 × 435 mm.
The Trustees of the British Museum, London
(1868-8-22-890)
(Hollstein, XLIII, no. 31)

Gainsborough's large-scale copy of the central panel of Rubens's great altarpiece (1611–1614, Antwerp Cathedral) was painted during his years in Bath. He had naturally not seen the original, and his copy was probably inspired by the modello (fig. 3) then nearby at Corsham Court, where he painted portraits of the Methuen family as well as a copy of a Van Dyck double portrait in that collection.

The unfinished state of the copy is further evidence of that inspiration; however, it is executed in reverse and must surely depend more immediately on Lucas Vorsterman's large engraving of 1620 which would have been readily available in England (cat. 9). According to Fulcher, Gainsborough followed a similarly indirect process when he made "a reduced copy of an engraving of Titian's *Cornaro Family*, begun from the print but finished from the picture."[1]

Fulcher reports further that "though he did not much attend to the works of the great historical painters of former ages, yet he was well aware that the language of the art – the art of imitation – must be learned somewhere ... he very judiciously applied himself to the Flemish School ... from that he learnt the harmony of colouring, the management and disposition of light and shadow."[2] He made several copies after Van Dyck's portraits,[3] and is also known to have copied Rubens's *Two Monks Reading* from his own collection.[4] No copies of Rubens's landscapes are known (although several were available to him in the original), but his copies after other Flemish landscapists include two versions from the late 1760s of David Teniers II's *The Return from Shooting* at Longford Castle and a copy (now lost) of a landscape by Pieter Bout and Adriaen Frans Boudewijns, then in the collection of his Bath physician, Dr. Charlton.[5]

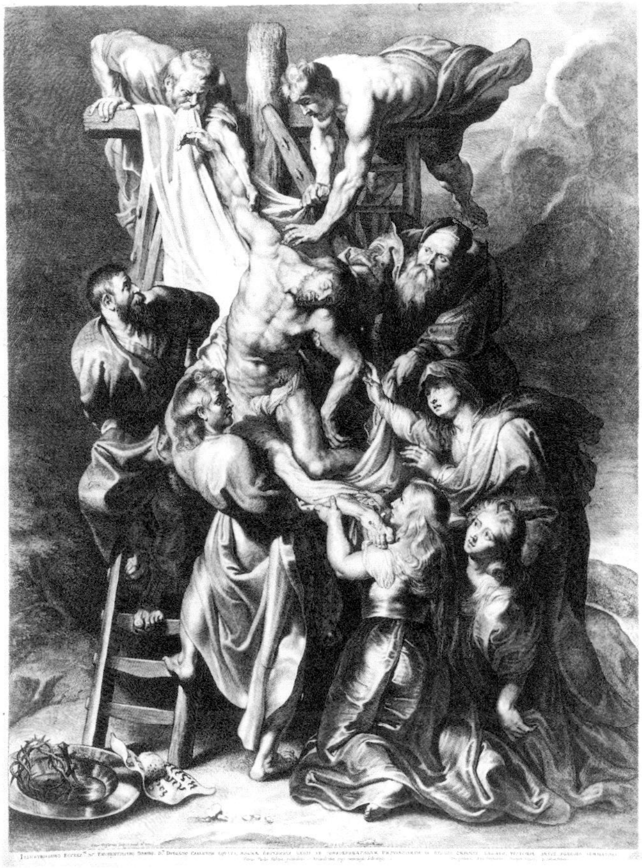

Cat. 9 Lucas Vorsterman after Rubens, *The Descent from the Cross*, The British Museum, London

Gainsborough's skill in retaining on canvas the spontaneity and luminosity of the original panel clearly reveals his absorption of Rubens's pictorial mastery. The high finish and highlighting of the figure of Christ contrasts dramatically with the summary execution and bold outlining of the secondary figures, set off by the brilliant white impasto of the winding-sheet that defines the composition's powerful diagonal axis.

The relationship, long recognised, between the figural group in the Barber *Harvest Wagon* and Gainsborough's copy after *The Descent from the Cross* is complex and has been questioned.[6] Clearly, the appeal of Rubens's composition for Gainsborough lay in its intricate structure, explored with such bravado in his copy, and not its subject (as he was not disposed to religious art). Individual figures from *The Descent from the Cross* are not transcribed into *The Harvest Wagon*, and the artist himself stated in a letter almost exactly contemporary with the *Harvest Wagon* that a landscape should never "be filled with History, or any figures but such as fill a place (I won't say stop a Gap) or [...] create a little business for the Eye to be drawn from the Trees in order to return to them with more glee."[7] Yet the *Harvest Wagon's* contrived and monumental figure-group was highly unusual for Gainsborough and indeed, is the most elaborate he ever attempted in a landscape. Its pyramidal composition and the downward tumble of its figures are mirrored in Rubens's picture, as is its strong white highlighting at the centre of the group, and its anchoring by brilliant red. Gainsborough has here assimilated – not appropriated – the structure of Rubens's *Descent*, and in so doing he transformed the tension and drama of the religious image into his most monumental pastoral painting to date. It is perhaps not surprising that when he returned to the theme some seventeen years later in the Toronto *Harvest Wagon* he should look again to Rubens, this time to *The Mired Cart* (cat. 16), whose vocabulary he similarly absorbed into his own powerful visual language.

1 Fulcher, p. 187.
2 Fulcher, pp. 162-163.
3 See cat. 7, note 5.
4 [Borenius], 1944, p. 109, no. 35. Gainsborough's copy is at the Ashmolean Museum, Oxford.
5 Hayes, p. 108 and nos. 92-93.
6 Michael Rosenthal, *British Landscape Painting*, Oxford 1982, p. 68.
7 Woodall, *Letters*, no. 49, p. 99.

10

Claude Gellée, *called* Lorrain (French, 1600-1682)

Pastoral Landscape

c. 1645

Oil on canvas, 101.5 × 134 cm.

Traces of signature and date lower right centre: *164[5?]*

The Trustees of the Barber Institute of Fine Arts,

The University of Birmingham

(Roethlisberger, no. 157)

[B]

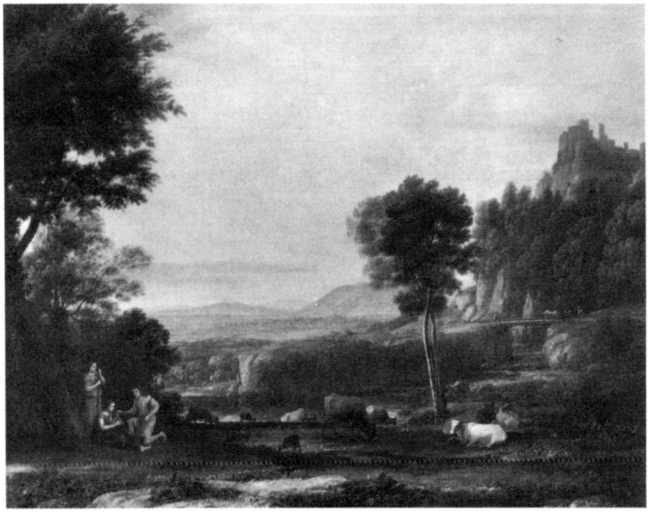

Cat. 10 Claude Lorrain, *Pastoral Landscape*, The Barber Institute of Fine Arts, The University of Birmingham

11
Claude Gellée, *called* Lorrain (French, 1600–1682).
The Embarkation of Carlo and Ubaldo
c. 1667
Oil on canvas, 92.7 × 138.4 cm.
Signed and inscribed lower left: *CLAVDIO G I ROMA*
Art Gallery of Ontario, Toronto, Gift of Group Captain H. L. Cooper, A.E.C., Salisbury, England, in appreciation of the contribution of Canadians in the Armed Services in the two World Wars, 1962 (62/12)
(Roethlisberger, no. 168)
[T]

The influence of French and Italian seventeenth-century predecessors was crucial for landscapists of Gainsborough's generation, both as a mould for artistic vision and as a point of reference for critics and connoisseurs. The works of Salvator Rosa, Nicolas Poussin and Gaspard Dughet – but above all of Claude – all contributed to Gainsborough's formulation of a grand manner in his own landscape style.

Claude's impact was pervasive among eighteenth-century British collectors and landscape painters: private holdings of his paintings (as well as his drawings and etchings) were stronger in Great Britain than anywhere else and all critics of consequence there, including Walpole, Price, Reynolds and Hazlitt, commented extensively on the artist's idyllic vision of nature and his unique treatment of light.

Pastoral Landscape was in the collection of Thomas Walker, Surveyor General, in 1741 and remained in English hands after his death in 1748. *Coast View with the Embarkation of Carlo and Ubaldo* was owned by Henry Grey, Duke of Kent, during the same period and remained with that family through the rest of the century. Gainsborough could have known these or numerous other landscapes then in England, as well as, of course, the engravings that further popularised Claude's paintings among artists and writers.[1]

The Claudean device of setting two groups of trees of different types and sizes at opposite sides of the picture to frame the figural group and to direct the eye towards the landscape lying beyond is adopted repeatedly by Gainsborough (as well as by his contemporaries) from the 1760s onwards, and finds its most eloquent expression in such paintings as *Rocky Wooded Landscape with Rustic Lovers* (cat. 14). Equally important to these and other landscapes of the 1760s and 1770s, including the Barber *Harvest Wagon*, is the glow of Claude's suffused light that tinges the entire landscape with golden warmth. It was, indeed, the special character of Claudean light that most attracted eighteenth-century comment: "The pictures of Claude are brilliant to a high degree ... that brilliancy is so diffused over the whole of them, so happily balanced, so mellowed and subdued by the almost visible atmosphere which pervades every part, and united all together, that nothing in particular catches the eye – the whole is splendour, the whole is repose..."[2]

1 *Pastoral Landscape*, for example, was engraved by François Vivares and published by Charles Knapton in 1741.
2 Uvedale Price, *An Essay on the Picturesque*, first publ. 1794, Edinburgh & London, 1842, p. 117.

12
Margaret Gainsborough
c. 1772
Oil on canvas, 75.6 × 62.9 cm.
Tate Gallery, London, presented by the family of Richard J. Lane, 1896
(Waterhouse, no. 280)

Margaret Gainsborough, shown here at the age of about 21, was the younger surviving daughter of the artist (see also cat. 5). He portrayed her either individually or with her sister on various occasions from the age of four, but this portrait is the one which most convincingly demonstrates that the features of the climbing girl in the Barber *Harvest Wagon* are hers. Both pictures show her in profile, and they were painted within a few years of each other. The resemblance is particularly apparent in the shape of the nose, colour of the hair and long neck with its ribbon necklet. On stylistic grounds, however, and especially on account of the impressionistic handling of the drapery, it is unlikely that this portrait preceded *The Harvest Wagon*, or should be regarded as a study for it.

Comparisons may be made with the bust length of many of Gainsborough's early works, eg. his self portrait of 1758/9 (cat. 4). However, *Margaret Gainsborough* is conceived as an oval picture within a picture, a format which Gainsborough used on numerous occasions from c. 1760. Yet in no other case did he link the space of the inner picture with the outer by flowing drapery, a connective device which recalls Hogarth's self-portrait with his Pug (1745, Tate Gallery, London). This link almost certainly has a symbolic dimension, signifying the close tie between artist and daughter, who shared her father's talent as an amateur musician.

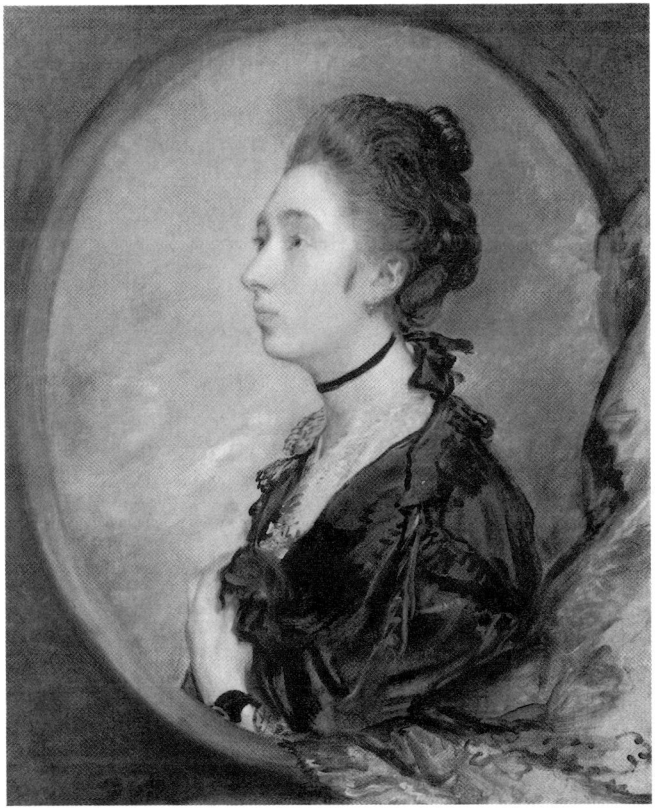

Cat. 12 Gainsborough, *Margaret Gainsborough*
Tate Gallery, London

13
Going to Market
c. 1768–71
Oil on canvas, 119.4 × 146.1 cm.
The Iveagh Bequest, Kenwood (English Heritage)
(Hayes, no. 95)

Going to Market is one of a number of large-scale landscapes by Gainsborough, dating from around 1770, which centre on groups of rustic travellers. Other examples are *Peasants going to Market, Early Morning* (formerly Royal Holloway College, Egham) and *The Road from Market* (Toledo Museum of Art).[1] It has been suggested that these themes of journeying reflect the disruption to the old certainties of rural existence which resulted from the wave of enclosures and engrossments of agricultural land taking place between 1760 and 1780.[2] Encroaching landlords often brought about the dispossession and migration of the poor, as lamented by Oliver Goldsmith in his poem, *The Deserted Village*, published in 1770. Gainsborough's own view of the countryside, however, as a place of beauty, grace and harmony, was traditional and was shared by many of his contemporaries. It had a long pedigree, stemming from the *Eclogues* of Virgil and other classical writings, but certainly assumed

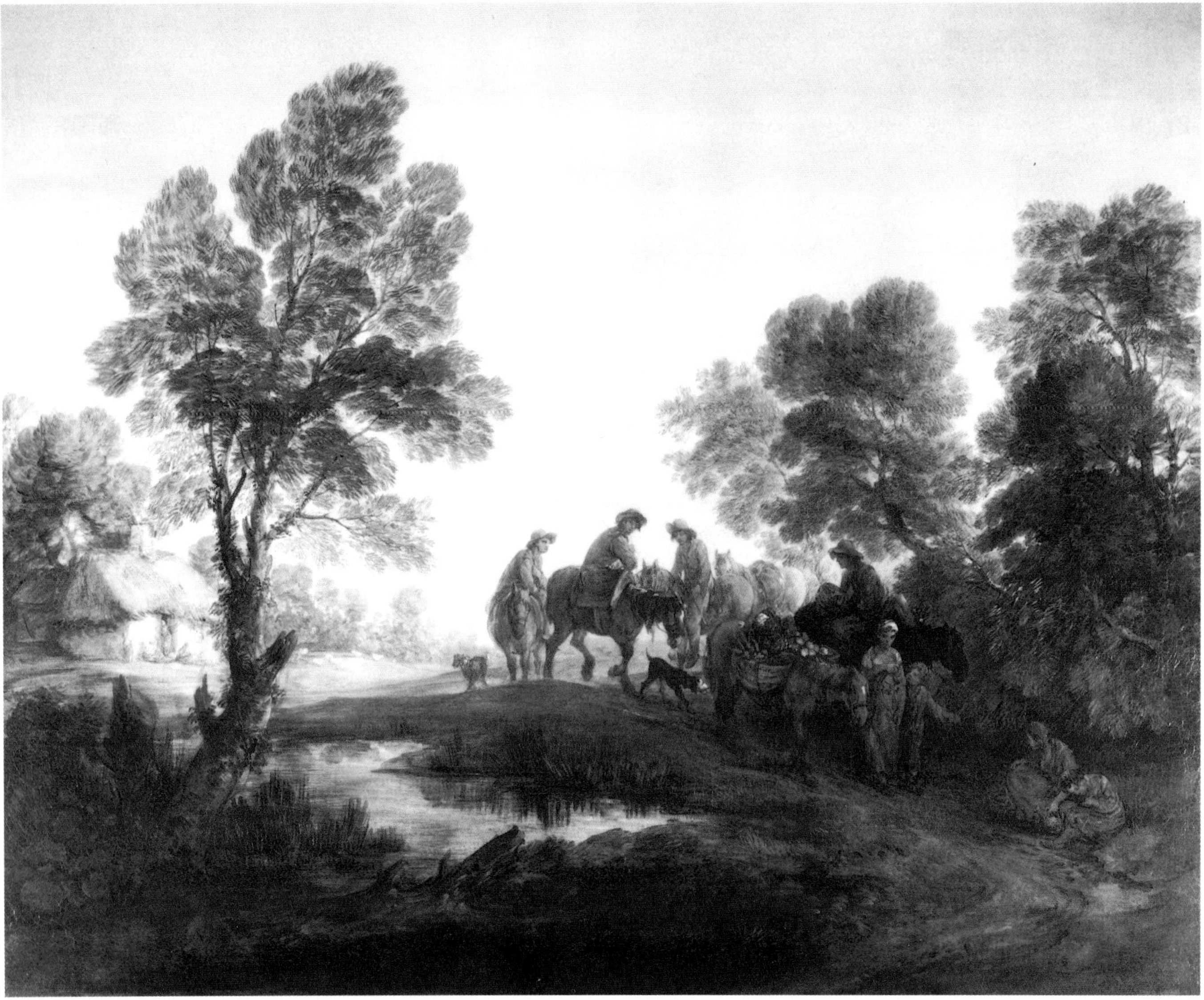

Cat. 13 Gainsborough, *Going to Market*
The Iveagh Bequest, Kenwood (English Heritage)

heightened poignancy and topicality in the face of the changes being effected in agrarian life by the Industrial Revolution.

There are a number of examples of the subject of peasants going to market in Dutch and Flemish seventeenth-century painting, by Frans Snyders, Philips Wouwermans and others. Figures appearing on the brow of a hill, with a brilliant dawn behind, are found in Aelbert Cuyp's *Muleteers in a Hilly Landscape* (Mauritshuis, The Hague).[3] *Going to Market* also has some compositional similarities to etchings by Claude of *The Flight into Egypt* and *The Departure for the Fields*.[4] The beautiful effect of the morning light, however, coupled with Gainsborough's employment of strong Baroque diagonals as structural axes of his composition, depend heavily on the example of Rubens in such a work as *The Birdcatchers* (Louvre, Paris). Parallels of composition, if not always of sentiment, may be made with French rococo landscape, notably Boucher's *Encounter on the Road* (Museum of Fine Arts, Springfield Mass.), a variant of which may have been known to Gainsborough.[5]

The grouping of the figures and horses in *Going to Market* provides a complex yet poetic alternative to the pyramidal arrangement of the Barber *Harvest Wagon*, to which it is almost exactly contemporary. The pictures share many compositional features, notably the pond surrounded by rushes and the large, decaying tree trunk in the foreground. The serene delicacy of the sky with its subtle modulation from smooth light blue to impastoed gold and mauve, however, contrasts with the agitated cloudiness of *The Harvest Wagon*. As observed by Hayes, the single, dominating tree at left is strongly influenced by the style of the Flemish painter, David Teniers II (1610–1690).[6] The hatched, spiky brush-strokes of its foliage contrast with the more fluent, rococo touches of that in *The Harvest Wagon*. Elsewhere there are some deliciously free passages, most notably the impressionistic treatment of the distant cottage chimney.

A marked tension is apparent between the clear, golden lighting which silhouettes the central group of figures and illuminates the cottage and distant pasture, and the dark shadows of the foreground. The contrast seems to set the peasants themselves between a world of iridescent beauty and ordered prosperity and the sombre, shiftless existence symbolised by the beggars to the right. The gesture of the younger of these, who is in the act of scratching her head, or removing a flea, suggests that they have just awoken from a night spent in the open air. The old woman's pitcher and basket are empty, in stark contrast to the paniers of the leading horse, laden with carrots, turnips, cauliflowers and potatoes. This emphasis on the role of honest labour in avoiding mendicity cannot have been accidental and is given added poignancy by the appeal of the leading boy to his older sister on the beggars' behalf – an appeal not graciously received.

In the background, the sun is striking the window of the cottage while a woman may be discerned entering, carrying more wood for the recently-lit fire. This was the first appearance of the motif of a family grouped outside a cottage door in Gainsborough's painting. Although it is here of minor importance, it became one of the artist's principal themes in the 1780s, eg. *The Woodcutter's Return* exhibited at the Royal Academy in 1782.[7] Gainsborough's interest in such subjects during his last decade may well account for the more informal grouping of figures in the Toronto *Harvest Wagon* in comparison with the Barber version. Gainsborough returned to travel subjects at intervals in his later career, eg. *Country Cart crossing a Ford* (c. 1782–4, Christchurch Mansion, Ipswich).[8] The final reprise of the market theme is to be found in *The Market Cart* (cat. 24).

Going to Market originally belonged to John, 2nd Viscount Bateman, of Shobdon Court, Herefordshire, a friend of Horace Walpole (cats. 26 and 27). Gainsborough presented Lord Bateman with a group of watercolour drawings in September 1770, and this suggests a similar date for the painting, which is supported by stylistic evidence.

1 Hayes, nos. 107 and 89 respectively.
2 Hayes, pp. 8–9, 148.
3 Dillian Gordon, *Second Sight. Rubens: The Watering Place. Gainsborough: The Watering Place*, exh. cat., National Gallery, London, 1981, p. 17.
4 Lino Mannocci, *The Etchings of Claude Lorrain*, New Haven and London, 1988, nos. 34 and 9 respectively.
5 Georges Wildenstein, *Les peintures de Fragonard*, Paris, 1960, no. 113. Attributed to Fragonard, this was no. 33 in the Earl of Pembroke sale, Paris, 30 June 1862; unfortunately its date of acquisition into the Pembroke collection is unknown.
6 Hayes, p. 439.
7 The Duke of Rutland, Belvoir Castle; Hayes, no. 105.
8 Hayes, no. 144.

14
Rocky Wooded Landscape with Rustic Lovers
[Plate IV, p. 13]
c. 1771–4
Oil on canvas, 119.4 × 147.3 cm.
Private Collection, United Kingdom
(Hayes, no. 113)

Painted a few years later than the Barber *Harvest Wagon*, this is without doubt one of the most beautiful and powerful of Gainsborough's landscapes from the late Bath period. The composition is consciously Claudean, with repoussoir groups of trees and hazy distant landscape providing a carefully modulated idyllic setting for the pastoral group of cows and goat to the left and the dallying couple to the right. The visual relationship of these figures is subtly reflected by the rhythm of the trees above, and by the interaction of the animals, which recall the work of Aelbert Cuyp. The opening to the distance is both emphasised and filled by a lone herdsman – a favourite motif of Gainsborough's – emerging over the crest of the bank.

Rustic lovers appear frequently in Gainsborough landscapes from the mid-1750s, eg. in *Wooded Landscape with Country Wagon, Milkmaid and Drover* (cat. 6), but here they are more idealised than in earlier works. The theme reaches an apogee in the 'fancy' *Haymaker and Sleeping Girl* of about 1785.[1] The picturesque rocks against which the present couple's courtship is enacted, however, are new as foreground features, and recall the wild terrains of Salvator Rosa (1615–73). They are more usually to be found in Gainsborough's later landscapes, particularly those which, like the Toronto *Harvest Wagon*, postdate the artist's 1783 visit to the Lake District. In the present case they are probably based on Gainsborough's drawings of Wick or Hampton Rocks, just outside Bath. Benjamin West would later praise the vicinity with great enthusiasm, commenting on "Rocks of the finest forms for a painter that He had ever seen [. . .] *Quarry's* worked out, now most picturesque and romantic. Wyck and Hampton rocks, Chedder Cliffs, most picturesque – distances the most beautiful".[2]

In contrast to the glowing, almost Turneresque yellow of the horizon, there are prominent areas of more forceful handling, both in the sky itself, where rough slabs of encrusted white, yellow and pink impasto have been laid on with the palette-knife, and in the rocks, which are enlivened with tints of yellow, pink and violet reflected from the setting sun. These areas are more highly worked than in the Barber *Harvest Wagon*. The use of a bright orange-red for emphasis was a feature of the artist's work at this time. Noticeable in the faces of the rustics and the girl's apron, it acts as eye-catcher and pictorial punctuation, a purpose also served by the red coat hanging from the chain in *The Harvest Wagon*.

A Grand Landscape, the traditional title as given on the frame, is of significance since, to Gainsborough's mind, landscape was the antithesis of the subject-matter suited to the 'grand style' promulgated by his rival, Reynolds, at the Royal Academy. Yet here he seems to make the landscape itself monumental, whereas in *The Harvest Wagon* it is the figures which capture the viewer's attention.

Rocky Wooded Landscape with Rustic Lovers was presented to Walter Wiltshire, together with the Barber *Harvest Wagon*, by Gainsborough when he left Bath in 1774. Prior to this the two paintings, which are almost exactly the same size, may have been exhibited together at the Royal Academy in 1771.[3]

1 Museum of Fine Arts, Boston, Mass.; Waterhouse, no. 815.
2 *The Diary of Joseph Farington*, VIII, ed. K. Cave, New Haven and London, 1982, p. 3138 (10 November 1807).
3 Gainsborough's two landscapes exhibited that year were nos. 79 and 80.

15
Francis Wheatley (1747–1801)
The Harvest Wagon [Plate V, p. 14]
1774
Oil on canvas, 128.3 × 101.6 cm.
Signed lower left: *F. Wheatley 1774*
City of Nottingham Museums, Castle Museum and Art Gallery

Wheatley worked mainly as a painter of small whole-length portraits and conversation pieces until he left London in 1779. In 1774, however, he began exhibiting landscapes, and executed this idiosyncratic and sophisticated variation of Gainsborough's *Harvest Wagon*. His picture is clearly based on the Barber version, which he could have seen when it was exhibited in London at the Society of Artists in 1767. Alternatively, if it was shown at the Royal Academy of 1771,[1] he could have seen it there. His interest in the subject may well have been stimulated by the arrival of Gainsborough in London in 1774.

A party of farmworkers are shown returning from the fields in a wagon during harvest-time. They are of both sexes and various ages, comprising two seated women and a girl, a standing woman and youth, a hatted and huddled old woman with her back to the viewer, and a hatted drover seated at the front. They have slowed in order to ask directions from a peasant on the road. On his back he carries a keg.

Wheatley's *Harvest Wagon* demonstrates the influence of Gainsborough on one of the rising young artists of the day. Wheatley is known to have owned at least one drawing of the market cart theme by Gainsborough.[2] In later years the influence was perhaps reciprocated, when Gainsborough's highly uncharacteristic *Diana and Actaeon* (1785, Buckingham Palace, Royal Collection) was possibly inspired by Wheatley's *Bathers by a Waterfall* (1783, Yale Center for British Art, New Haven).[3] *Wooded Landscape with Peasants, Country Carts, Faggot-gatherers and Barn* (cat. 23) also shows marked compositional similarities to Wheatley's *Harvest Wagon*.

The differences between the paintings by Gainsborough and Wheatley are as significant as their similarities. Wheatley's wagon is more clearly connected with the harvest (as opposed to haymaking) than Gainsborough's, even though there is no sign of harvesting in the fields lying in the distance. It contains straw, and one ear of barley is visible below the seated woman on the left. Wheatley has taken the wagon and the pyramid of figures from Gainsborough, but his format is vertical and the landscape, especially in the background, is more specific, seeming to depict an observed location. The figure composition is gentler, less thrusting and more anecdotal, while still reflecting Gainsborough's ideas in many details, such as the raised rake, the cider barrel and the grey horse, now moved to the back of the row. The climbing woman, however, has been eliminated in favour of the more static and rugged male peasant, and the costumes of the women are less idealised.

A number of the changes themselves prefigure Gainsborough's own compositional adaptations made in the later Toronto *Harvest Wagon*, such as the prominence of the tall bare tree in the left foreground – a Ruisdaelian motif more commonly used by Gainsborough in his early work. The grouping of the trees to the right is also recalled in Gainsborough's later picture, but the most obvious connection between the two works is Gainsborough's more casual reorganisation of his figures and the inclusion of children in the seated group of women in his wagon. Unlike Wheatley, however, Gainsborough preserved the motif of the woman being helped up by a leaning man.

Although Wheatley did produce other rustic genre scenes, including *The Hay Cart*,[4] the fact that he never seems to have attempted another landscape on such a scale as this defines it as special within his oeuvre. It must have been to some extent experimental, reflecting the influence of Richard Wilson in the foliage of the silhouetted trees and Neoclassical prototypes in the youth shown in profile. Lighting, colour and impastoed details distinguish Wheatley's painting from Gainsborough's, yet it is impossible not to think of Gainsborough when observing such details as the prominent burdock plant featured at the lower right.

1 See p. 10 and cat. 14, note 3.
2 Hayes, *Drawings*, no. 464.
3 Hayes, p. 539. The painting, also known as *Salmon Leap at Leixlip with Nymphs Bathing*, was engraved by R. Pollard and F. Jukes in 1785.
4 Government Art Collection of the United Kingdom; Mary Webster, *Francis Wheatley*, New Haven and London, 1970, no. 71.

16
After Peter Paul Rubens (Flemish, 1577–1640)
The Mired Cart
Oil on canvas, 87 x 129 cm.
Private Collection, United Kingdom

17
Schelte Adamsz. Bolswert (Flemish, c. 1586–1659)
The Mired Cart (after Rubens)
1635–40
Engraving, 330 x 447 mm.
The Trustees of the British Museum, London
(1891-4-14-1277)
(Hollstein, III, no. 309)

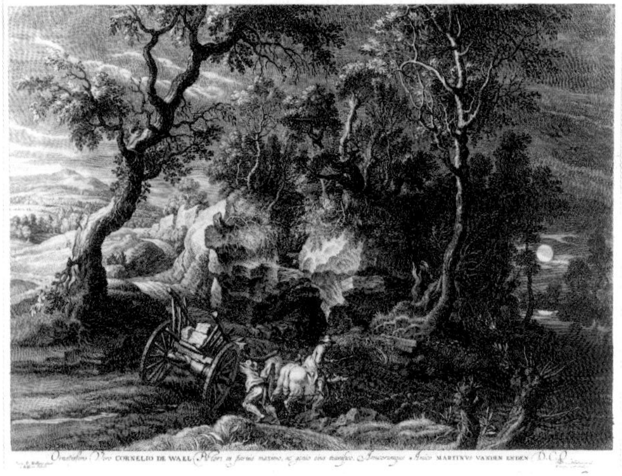

Cat. 17 Schelte Adamsz. Bolswert (after Rubens), *The Mired Cart*, The British Museum, London

18
John Browne (1719–1790)
The Waggoner (after Rubens)
1776
Engraving, 428 × 572 mm.
The Trustees of the British Museum, London (S.233.53.5)

Of the several landscape paintings by Rubens in English collections during the eighteenth century, *The Mired Cart* of c. 1618, then in the collection of Sir Robert Walpole and now in the Hermitage, St. Petersburg (see cats. 26 and 27) was probably the best known. It had been described by Horace Walpole in his extensive catalogue of his father's collection at Houghton Hall,[1] as well as in his *Anecdotes of Painting in England*.[2]

Four painted copies of the composition are recorded. One was in the collection of Viscount Harcourt at Nuneham Park, Oxford (cat. 16), and like the Walpole picture, may also have been known to Gainsborough.[3] The remaining three are untraced, but have been in continental collections during this century and are not known to have been earlier in England.[4]

In addition, *The Mired Cart* composition was well known through engravings by Schelte Adamsz. Bolswert and John Browne (cats. 17 and 18). The latter is dated 1776 and was engraved from a drawing by Joseph Farington after the original painting while it was at Houghton Hall.[5] There is no record of Gainsborough seeing either print, but the Bolswert engraving had circulated widely in England. Indeed, a print was at Houghton Hall and is included in Walpole's *Aedes Walpolianae* with a drawing of *The Mired Cart* then attributed to Rubens, purchased from Mariette's collection and acquired by Robert Walpole in 1776.[6]

While evidence of Gainsborough's familiarity with Rubens's *Mired Cart* composition is circumstantial, we do know that he admired Rubens's paintings, and that in one instance he copied a Rubens composition and used it in the creation of the first version of his *Harvest Wagon* (cat. 8). This was the central grouping of *The Descent from the Cross*, for which an oil sketch was in England but for which he clearly relied on the reversed composition in Vorsterman's engraving (cat. 9). Similarly, the analogies between *The Mired Cart* and the Toronto *Harvest Wagon* suggest that

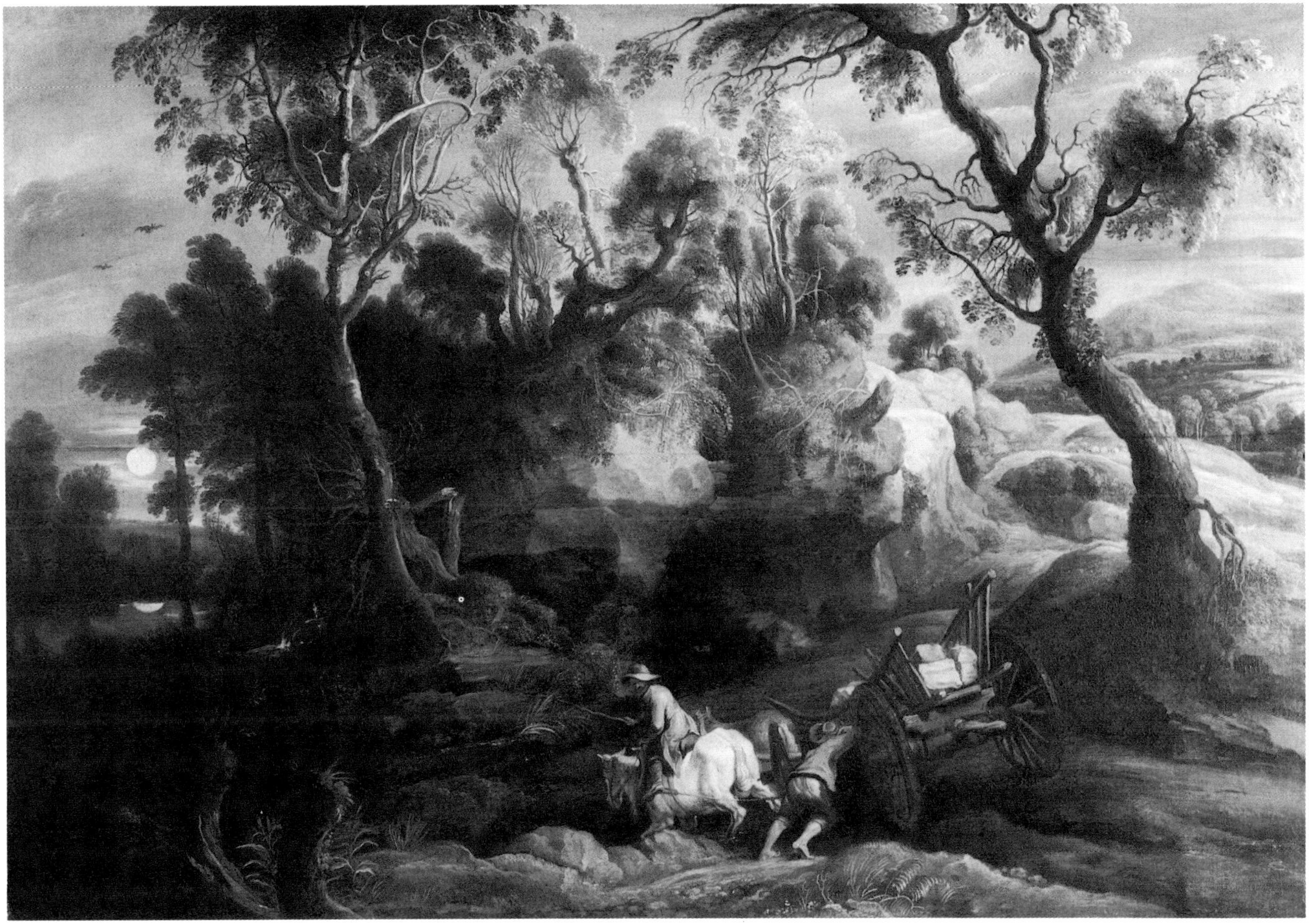

Cat. 16 After Rubens, *The Mired Cart*
Private Collection, United Kingdom

here, too, he relied on a print source. The angled cart moving from left to right, the rocky extrusion behind it, the figure to the right with arms raised and the gnarled tree to the left are all mirrored in the engravings. Hayes has suggested that Gainsborough's knowledge of Rubens's modello for the *Descent* provided the inspiration for his subsequent copy of the print after the same motif.[7] It is tempting to speculate that the influence of *The Mired Cart* on *The Harvest Wagon* was similarly driven by both the painting and engraving.

1 Horace Walpole, *Aedes Walpolianae*, fol. 53v.
2 Horace Walpole, *Anecdotes of Painting in England*, II, Strawberry Hill, 1762, p. 85.
3 The picture was described by Reynolds and Walpole in a catalogue they compiled of the pictures at Nuneham and was left with Reynolds in London for restoration (Hayes, p. 123, note 54).
4 Wolfgang Adler, *Corpus Rubenianum Ludwig Burchard; Part XVIII: Landscapes and Hunting Scenes. I: Landscapes*, London, 1982, under no. 19.
5 Providence (RI), Brown University, Bell Gallery, *Rubenism*, 1975, cat. 6.
6 Julius Held, *Rubens; Selected Drawings*, London, 1959, I, p. 34. In addition, the plates for the fifth and final state of the engraving are in England (F. W. H. Hollstein, *Dutch and Flemish Etchings, Engravings and Woodcuts*, Amsterdam, 1949-, III, p. 89).
7 Hayes, p. 107.

19
Gainsborough Dupont (1754–1797)
George, Prince of Wales
Oil on canvas, 76 × 63 cm.
Washington (DC), National Gallery of Art, Andrew W. Mellon Collection (1937.1.98)
[T]

20
John Raphael Smith (1752–1812)
George, Prince of Wales (after Gainsborough)
1783
Mezzotint, 663 x 459 mm.
The Hon. C. A. Lennox-Boyd
(Frankau, no. 358)
[B]

21
Mrs. Fitzherbert
1784
Oil on canvas, 76 × 63.5 cm.
The Fine Arts Museums of San Francisco, Mildred Anna Williams Collection (1941.19)
(Waterhouse, no. 254)
[T]

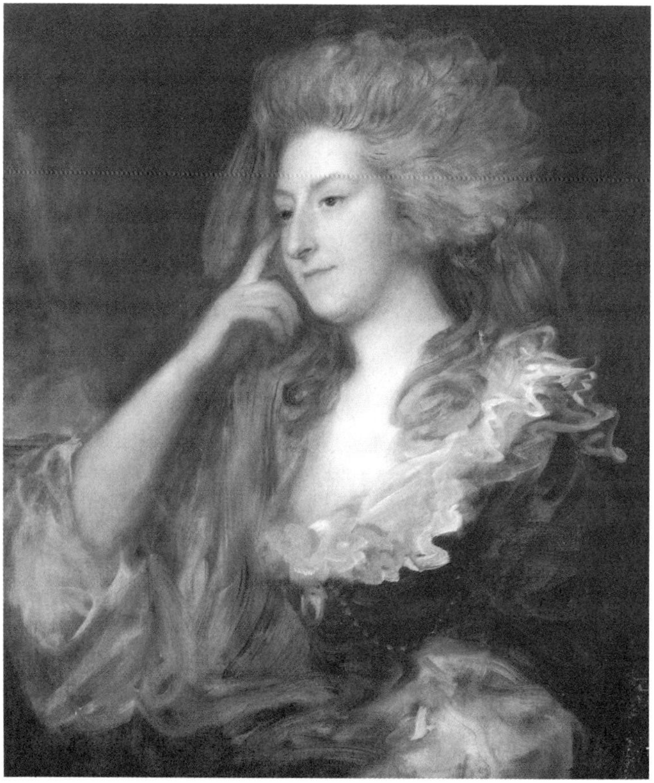

Cat. 21 Gainsborough, *Mrs. Fitzherbert*
The Fine Arts Museums of San Francisco

22
Richard Cosway (1742–1821)
Mrs. Fitzherbert
Watercolour and pencil, 122 × 73 mm.
The Earl of Yarmouth, Ragley Hall
[B]

Traditionally, the Toronto *Harvest Wagon* has been known as a commission from the Prince of Wales, and is one of two landscapes he gave as a pair to Mrs. Fitzherbert in 1810. Certainly, the Prince had acquired the *Harvest Wagon* by April 1786, and the other picture, *Rocky Wooded Upland Landscape* (fig. 6) by July 1784. Hayes accepts the identification of the latter picture as a princely commission, but not the Toronto landscape, which he concludes was purchased by the Prince from the artist soon after its execution. The landscapes (which have little in common thematically or stylistically) are recorded as a commissioned pair in 1789 and again in 1841, each time in the context of sales, and the temptation to reinforce their aristocratic connection may have led to an exaggeration of fact.[1]

The Prince of Wales (cats. 19 and 20) was, at any rate, a passionate collector from an early age and his reputation for free spending was well known and much criticised.[2] Until their relationship ended in 1808, his first adviser in picture collecting was the artist Richard Cosway, whose foppish and fashionable *persona* well suited the Prince's hedonistic tastes. Under Cosway's guidance and while still in his early twenties the Prince assembled a collection primarily of seventeenth and eighteenth-century Italian pictures.[3] During the same period he cultivated his interest in contemporary British art, and it is not surprising that he turned to his friend for a miniature of his mistress (cat. 22), Maria Anne Fitzherbert (née Smythe, 1756–1837).

The Harvest Wagon and *Rocky Wooded Upland Landscape* were among fifteen Gainsboroughs the Prince had acquired by 1797. Six were portraits of himself, including one exhibited at the Royal Academy in 1782 that was hugely popular (now Waddesdon Manor) and generated, amongst other works, Smith's mezzotint (cat. 20) and Gainsborough Dupont's copy of the head and shoulders (cat. 19). The portrait and the two landscapes, as well as the unfinished *Mrs. Fitzherbert* (cat. 21) were among the thirteen pictures listed in a bill, probably prepared by Gainsborough's widow, that was paid in 1793 at the settlement of the Prince's enormous debts.[4] Farington records that "the first time when the debts of the Prince were to be liquidated Notice was given for creditors to send an acct. of their demands. The Prince then owed Gainsborough Money, who said the Prince had always behaved in a gentlemanly manner to him, therefore the Trustees should never see a demand of his."[5] As Oliver Millar has observed, the artist's reluctance to acknowledge the Prince's obligation testifies to the depth of their friendship.[6]

The Prince's long relationship with Mrs. Fitzherbert, punctuated by their secret marriage in 1785, was the source of public and political disapproval and was lampooned frequently in contemporary caricature. She was older than the Prince, Roman Catholic, twice widowed and her political allegiances were thought dangerous; their union was deemed illegal and the Prince was married to the more acceptable Princess Caroline of Brunswick in 1795.

The context for the Prince's acquisition of the two landscapes cannot be confidently ascertained. If they were not acquired together, they seem to have been paired soon after, and are cited as such in all references to the Prince's collection and later, Mrs. Fitzherbert's. Their acquisition – and the commission of Mrs. Fitzherbert's portrait – at around the time of the marriage might be significant, and although (like many of the Prince's pictures, including *Mrs. Fitzherbert*[7]) they languished in store at Carlton House, the eventual gift to his companion may well reflect an intention formed many years earlier.

1 For a detailed discussion of the early association of these pictures with the Prince of Wales, see pp. 27–29 in this catalogue.
2 The breadth of his collecting activity – and his stupendous expenditures – are documented in exh. cat, London, Buckingham Palace, The Queen's Gallery, *Carlton House; The Past Glories of George IV's Palace*, 1991–1992.
3 Stephen Lloyd, 'Forming the Taste of a Prince; Richard Cosway and George IV's Early Collecting,' *Apollo*, CXXXVIII, September 1993, pp. 192–194.
4 Ellis K. Waterhouse, 'A Gainsborough Bill for the Prince of Wales,' *Burlington Magazine*, LXXXVIII, November 1946, p. 276, nos. 5, 10–12.

5 *The Diary of Joseph Farington*, IV, ed. K. Garlick and A. Macintyre, New Haven and London, 1979, pp. 1146–1147 (25 January 1799).
6 *The Later Georgian Pictures in the Collection of Her Majesty the Queen*, London, 1969, p. xxvi.
7 Millar, 1969, p. 35. *Mrs. Fitzherbert* was commissioned in May 1784, "delivered unfinished by His Highness's orders" and eventually delivered to the sitter in 1830. (According to Waterhouse, the delivery was made by William IV in 1837; Waterhouse, 1946, p. 276).

23

Wooded Landscape with Peasants, Country Carts, Faggot-gatherers and Barn
c. 1784-5
Oil on canvas, 128 × 102.6 cm.
The Fine Arts Museums of San Francisco,
Roscoe and Margaret Oakes Collection (75.2.8)
(Hayes, no. 156)
[T]

Traditionally dated c. 1778, this picture is described by Hayes as close to the Toronto *Harvest Wagon* in tonality and brushwork and is dated by him to the same period as the latter picture. The central motif of the wagon moving away from the picture plane was of course already well established in Gainsborough's repertory, appearing as early as c. 1746–7 (see cat. 3), in drawings (cat. 31), and gloriously culminating, first, in the Barber *Harvest Wagon*. But as Hayes has shown, Gainsborough actually transcribed the two carts, staffage and much of the landscape structure of the San Francisco landscape directly from a picture by the seventeenth-century Dutch painter Pieter Molijn.[1] Thus, while in general terms the early influence on Gainsborough of Dutch painting was supplanted in the 1760s by his increasing interest in eighteenth-century French models and by the growing impact of Rubens, it is clear that even towards the end of his life, Gainsborough never forgot the lessons he absorbed during his youthful career, and that despite the crafting of a repertory and style uniquely his own well before the 1780s, he remained perfectly capable of direct appropriation at this late date.

The vertical format of this picture is itself unusual in Gainsborough's landscapes, one rare exception being the extraordinary *Market Cart* of 1786/7 (cat. 24). Despite his obvious reliance on a Dutch source (whose format is actually almost square), we should not overlook the more generic similarities of the San Francisco landscape to Francis Wheatley's *Harvest Wagon* of 1774 (cat. 15), whose proportions are identical and whose compositional structure is similar.

A painting in the Victoria Art Gallery, Bath, by Thomas Barker shows the artist seated at an easel with his teacher Charles Spackman looking on.[2] According to Hayes, Barker's principal source for his landscapes was Gainsborough and indeed, numerous works by Barker have traditionally been given to Gainsborough. Hayes has identified several paintings by Barker that are clearly modelled after his works (see cat. 25).[3] To these we might add the unidentified landscape on the easel in the picture at Bath, which looks surprisingly like the San Francisco landscape.

1 Hayes, p. 164 and pl. 196.
2 Exhibited 1790; Hayes, pl. 325.
3 Hayes, pp. 275–277.

24

The Market Cart [Plate VI, p. 16]
1786/7
Oil on canvas, 184 × 153 cm.
The Trustees of the National Gallery, London
(Hayes, no. 183)

One of the greatest of Gainsborough's late landscapes, *The Market Cart* is also the climax of the cart theme in the artist's oeuvre, which it amalgamates with the subject of peasants going to or from market. Reputedly, it was painted using motifs drawn during a visit to Lulworth Castle which Gainsborough made during a stay in the West Country in 1782.[1]

The influence of Claude is evident in the grouping of repoussoir trees at the left, and especially in the mountainous distance, comparable with that in the Barber *Harvest*

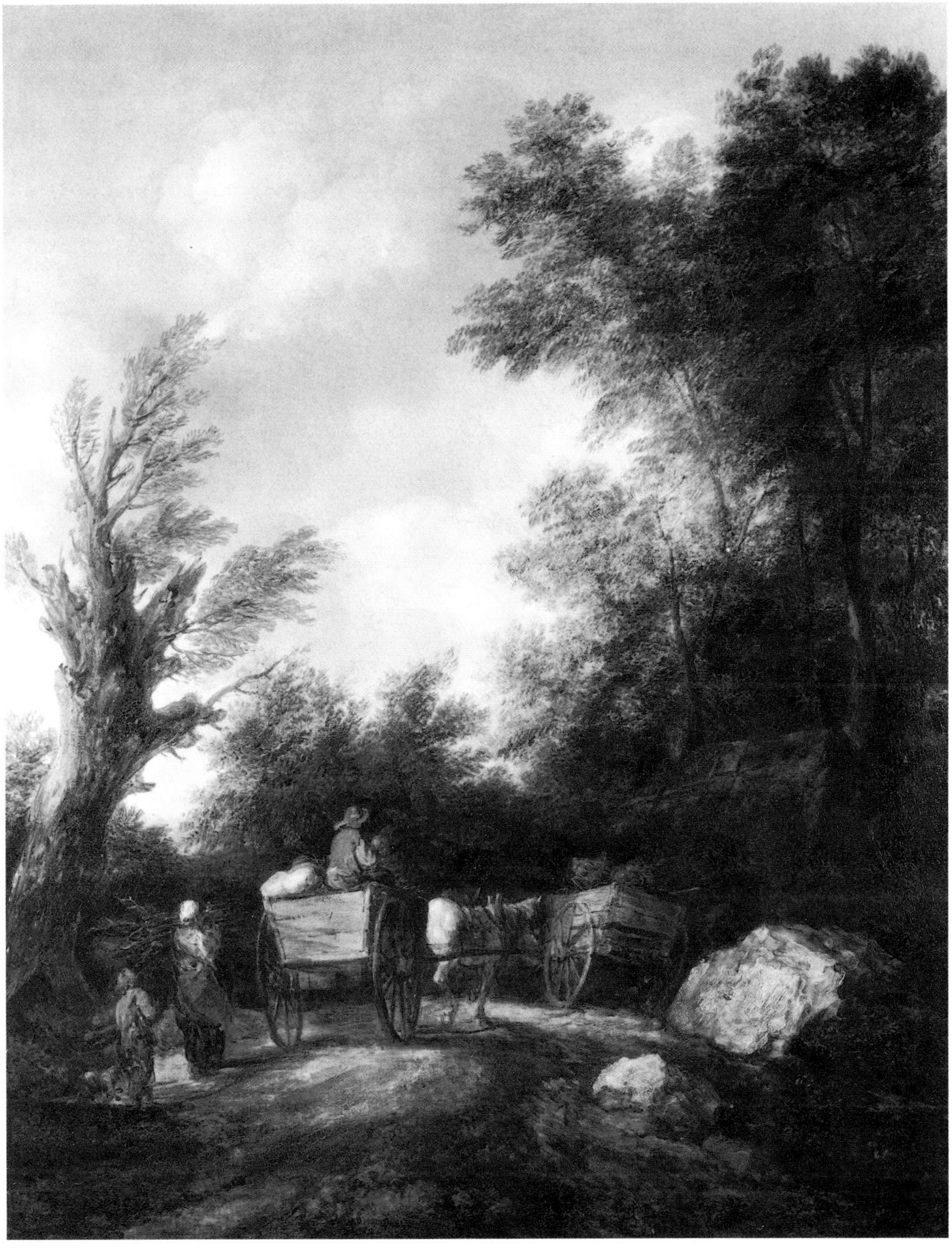

Cat. 23 Gainsborough, *Wooded Landscape with Peasants, Country Carts, Faggot-gatherers and Barn*, The Fine Arts Museums of San Francisco

Wagon. The great bank of trees, however, recalls the dense screen of foliage in the *Wooded Landscape with Country Wagon, Milkmaid and Drover* of almost twenty years before (cat. 6), as does the unusual vertical format. Compositionally, *The Market Cart* has affinities with both versions of *The Harvest Wagon.* As in the Barber *Harvest Wagon,* a grey horse features prominently in the picture but, in the present case, has been altered – now visibly – in the region of the head so as to give it additional direction and thrust. The feathery foliage of the tree at the left, and the pond at the lower right also recall the Barber picture. The less monumental grouping of the women on the cart, however, and the presence of a dog near the cart, are closer to the Toronto version, which predates *The Market Cart* by only a year or two. These two paintings are also closer in technique.

The cart is laden with autumnal produce – turnips, carrots and apples – which is here displayed more prominently than anywhere else in the artist's work. The faggot-gatherer was a favourite motif of Gainsborough's during the 1780s, appearing for example in the soft ground etching, *Wooded Landscape with Country Cart and Figures* (cat. 39). His prominence here and the picturesque qualities of the peasants also relate *The Market Cart* to the cottage-door pictures of the 1780s, while the naturalism of the scene and the red jacket of the boy look forward to the style of Constable.

The Market Cart was one of Gainsborough's last works.[2] Painted late in 1786, though the woodman and faggots were added early the following year, it was exhibited at Schomberg House, Pall Mall, in December 1786, and purchased by Sir Peter Burrell, later 1st Lord Gwydyr in May 1787.[3]

1 W. T. Whitley, Letter to *The Times*, 3 September 1929.
2 Its pendant, *Cottage Door with a Peasant Smoking* (University of Southern California, Los Angeles; Hayes, no. 185) was Gainsborough's last landscape of importance.
3 At the Gwydyr sale of 8–9 May 1829, it was bought by the Governors of the British Institution, who presented it to the National Gallery the following year. Its present title first occurred in the National Gallery catalogue of 1830.

25
Thomas Barker (1769–1847)
Landscape with Country Cart
Oil on canvas, 71.5 × 91.4 cm.
The Toledo Museum of Art, Gift of Arthur J. Secor (33.163)
[T]

Like many works by Barker, this picture was long attributed to Gainsborough, and has been given to the lesser artist by Hayes.[1] As he has noted, Barker's career hinged mainly on his ability to interpret Gainsborough's style, a talent that was already noted in 1809 by the watercolourist Thomas Hearne, who observed that "Barker's [landscapes] . . . were but Pasticcots from Gainsborough, and mannered."[2]

Landscape with Country Cart is a copy, much simplified, of the Toronto *Harvest Wagon,* and employs the same broad outlines of the composition. The landscape setting, complete with rocky extrusion, curved tree trunk and thick mass of foliage is taken directly from Gainsborough's painting, while the background has been reduced to a flat plain and large mountain. The principal figures – all women – again draw loosely on Gainsborough's complex

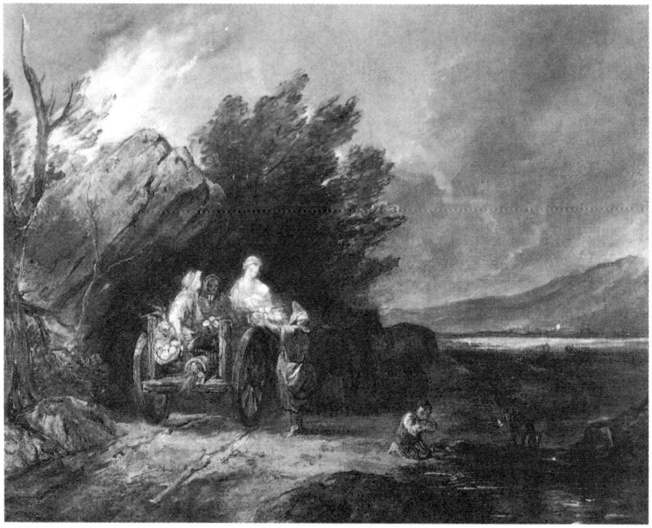

Cat. 25 Thomas Barker, *Landscape with Country Cart*
Toledo Museum of Art, Ohio

arrangement, with one seated figure cast in shadow and the most prominent cradling her infant with head turned. All the dynamism of Gainsborough's massing of forms has been lost: the young girl climbing into the cart has become a woman resting a basket on the wheel, and the spatial relationships among the figures crowded on the cart are ambiguous. Most important, the theme of the picture has changed: in Barker's canvas, the women have collected baskets of flowers, in a setting that seems inappropriate to such a harvest. The moral resonance of Gainsborough's painting – emphasising the rewards of labour and the strength of family ties – is here prettified, and the overriding vacuousness of its sentiment suggests an early nineteenth century date for this picture.

1 Hayes, p. 278.
2 Hearne to Farington, quoted in Hayes, ibid.

26
Joshua Reynolds (1723–1792)
Horace Walpole
1756
Oil on canvas, 127 × 102.9 cm.
Art Gallery of Ontario, Toronto, Bequest of John Paris Bickell, Toronto, 1952 (51/36)
[T]

27
Joshua Reynolds (1723–1792)
Horace Walpole
1757
Oil on canvas, 127 × 101.6 cm.
Signed and dated lower left: *J. Reynolds 1757*
The Earl of Yarmouth, Ragley Hall
[B]

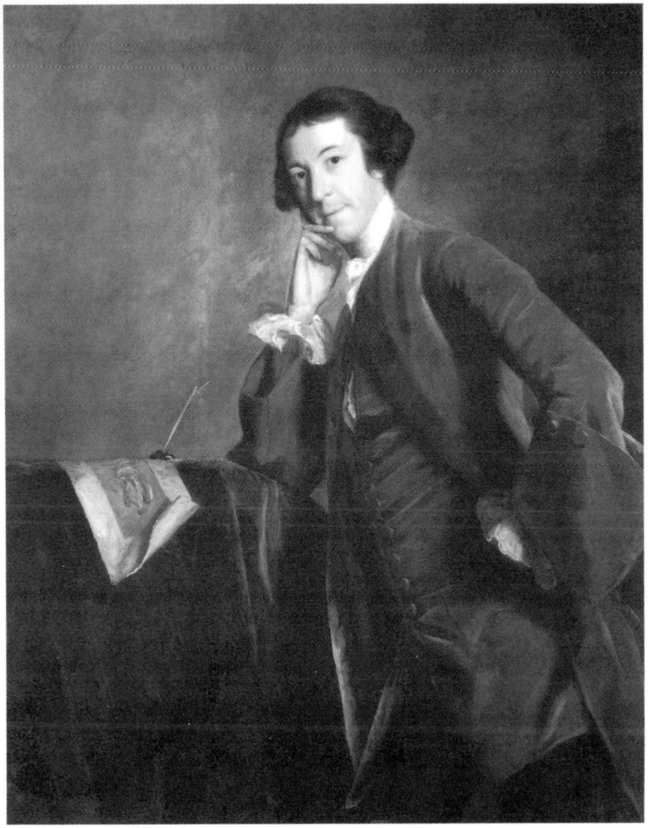

Cat. 26 Joshua Reynolds, *Horace Walpole*
Art Gallery of Ontario, Toronto

Reynolds painted at least two portraits of Walpole. The Toronto version (cat. 26) is the first, painted in 1756, and given by Walpole to his half-sister Lady Mary Churchill and her husband. He gave the second version, signed and dated 1757 (cat. 27), to his cousin, Francis Seymour Conway (later 1st Marquess of Hertford) around the end of that year. A third version at Bowood, traditionally thought to be autograph, is not recorded in the artist's pocket-books.[1] The Toronto and Ragley Hall versions are alike save for the print, reversed in the second picture.

The subject is shown leaning casually against a draped table, looking squarely at the viewer and with his right hand posed pensively against his cheek. Reynolds has perfectly captured that mixture of curiosity and erudition in Walpole's expression for which this remarkable man of letters was so well known. The book, manuscript, inkpot, quill and print of a Roman eagle (the sculpture was in Walpole's collection at Strawberry Hill) leave no doubt as to the sitter's chief passions: writing, collecting and antiquarianism.

Walpole was the youngest son of the politician Sir Robert Walpole, 1st Earl of Orford, whose formidable collection of pictures Gainsborough may well have known.[2] It numbered over four hundred pictures, including Rubens's *Mired Cart* (see cats. 16-18) which was sold in 1779 by Horace's nephew George Walpole, 3rd Earl of Orford, with almost half the collection, to the Empress Catherine II of Russia.[3]

The great critical impact of Walpole's *Anecdotes of Painting in England* (first published in 1762–1771) on English artists and collectors of his generation would have been felt by Gainsborough. In it, the author praises Rubens especially for his landscapes and for the universal appeal of his works: "His pictures were equally adapted to please the ignorant and the connoisseurs. Familiar subjects, familiar histories, treated with great lustre and fullness of colouring, a richness of nature and propriety of draperies, recommend themselves at first sight to the eyes of the vulgar. The just boldness of his drawing ... and attention to every part of his compositions ...; all this union of happy excellencies endears the work of Rubens to the best judges; he is perhaps the single artist who attracts the suffrages of every rank."[4] The taste for Rubens's pictures had remained strong in England since the artist's sojourn there in 1629.[5] Yet for Walpole, interest had clearly shifted away from the complex allegories and religious imagery for which he was celebrated. "Rubens was never greater than in landscape," he wrote, and in them he was "at least equal" to Titian.[6] The compositional analogies between Rubens's *Mired Cart* and the Toronto version of Gainsborough's *Harvest Wagon* suggest that for Gainsborough, too, Rubens's achievement lay in his ability to communicate values through landscape that touched the simple and sophisticated viewer in ways that high-minded history painting could not.

1 London, Royal Academy of Arts, *Reynolds*, cat. N. Penny et al., 1986, no. 28. For the third portrait, see also W. S. Lewis, *Horace Walpole*, Bollingen Series XXXV-9, New York, 1960, p. 137, where it is said to have been painted in 1761.
2 Hayes, p. 107.
3 Andrew Moore, "La collection de sir Robert Walpole," in: Dijon, Musée des Beaux-Arts, *L'Age d'or flamand et hollandais; collection de Catherine II, Musée de l'Ermitage, Saint-Pétersbourg*, 1993, pp. 65–71.
4 Horace Walpole, *Anecdotes of Painting in England*, II, Strawberry Hill, 1762, p. 78.
5 The history of the taste in England for Rubens's paintings is traced by Christopher White, 'Rubens and British Art 1630–1790,' in: *'Sind Briten hier?'; Relations between British and Continental Art 1680-1880*, Munich, 1981, pp. 27–43.
6 Walpole, 1762, p. 81.

28

Figure Study for the Barber *Harvest Wagon*

Black and white chalks on grey-blue paper, 249 × 286 mm.
Private Collection, United Kingdom
(Hayes, *Drawings*, no. 825)

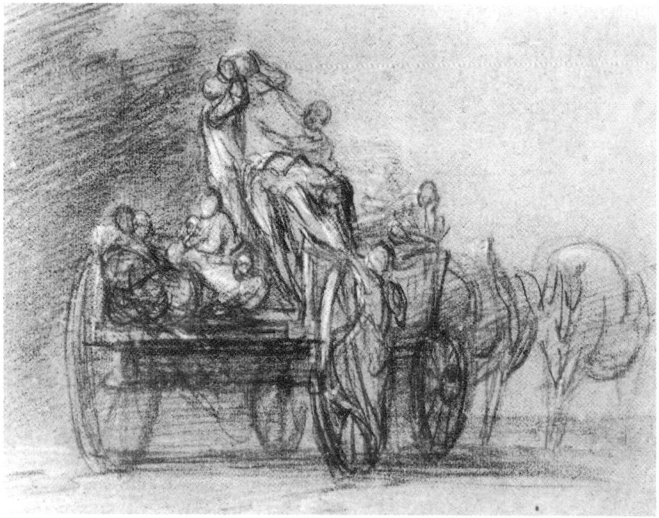

Cat. 28 Gainsborough, *Figure Study for The Harvest Wagon*
Private Collection, United Kingdom

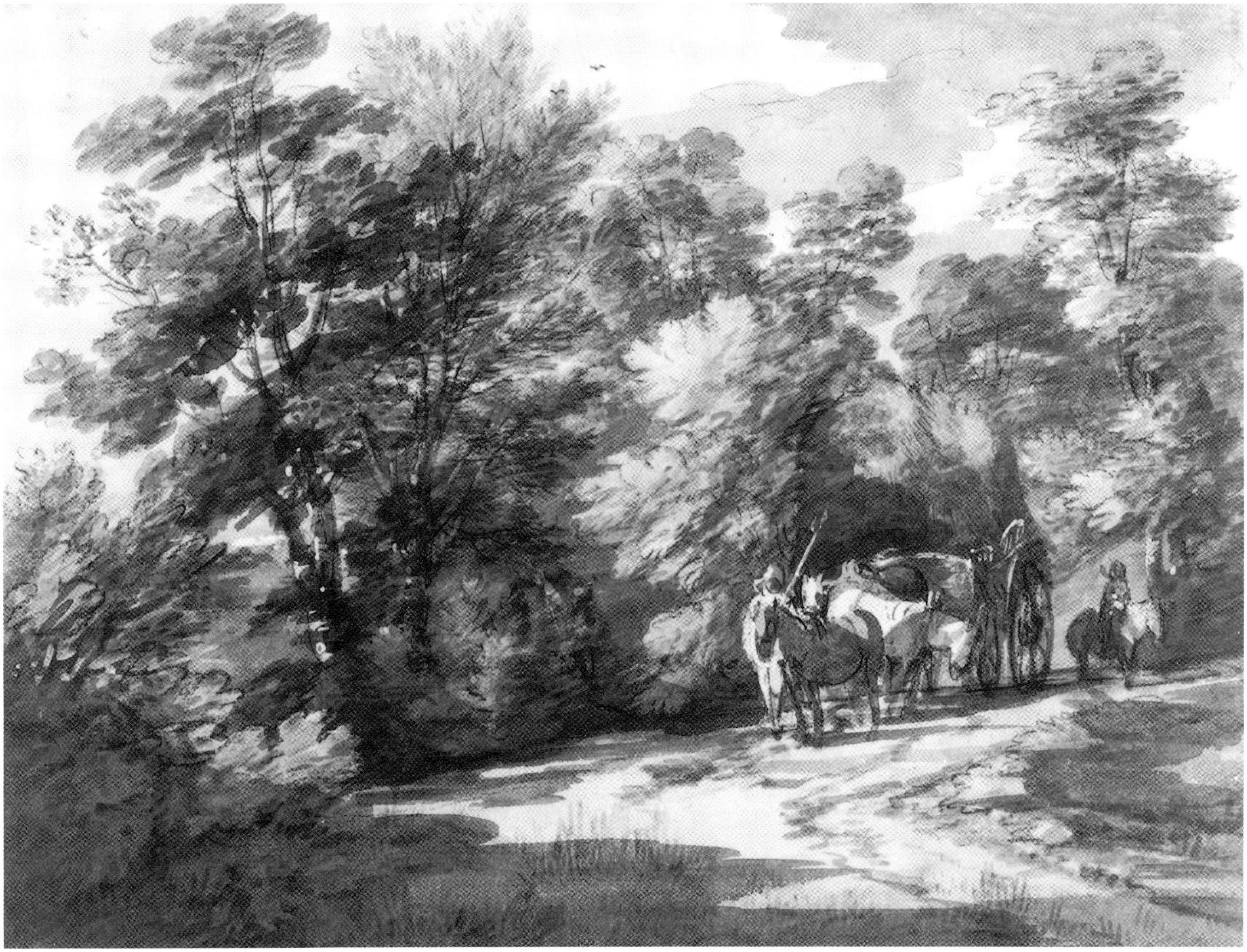

Cat. 30 *Wooded Landscape with Wagon in a Glade*
The British Museum, London

29

Study of a Harvest Wagon

Black and white chalks on grey-green paper, 146 × 202 mm.
Private Collection, United Kingdom
(Hayes, *Drawings*, no. 284)

Though undated, cat. 28 is a figure study for the Barber *Harvest Wagon* and should probably be assigned to c. 1767. Its close relationship to the finished composition is unusual in Gainsborough's drawings, and in it we can see that the artist has already resolved the general structure of the pyramidal group of figures, with two vying for their drink and the young man reaching over the side of the cart to help his companion climb the wheel. The position of the arms of the peasant seated towards the front of the cart is reversed.

Despite the close relationship of this drawing to the 1767 version of the *Harvest Wagon*, it is likely that Gainsborough referred back to it when he took up the theme again in 1784. The drawing includes a pair of mother and child groups seated at the rear of the cart; these are absent from the Barber picture (there replaced by two seated women positioned differently) but appear in much the same poses in the Toronto version. Similarly, the head of the horse nearest the cart looks straight ahead as in the drawing, whereas it droops in the Barber picture.

Cat. 29 is a study from nature from one of Gainsborough's sketch-books, and shows the harvest wagon from the same angle as the Barber and Toronto pictures. That he was more interested in establishing certain structural details and a particular viewpoint for eventual use in a painted work might be suggested by the absence of the rearmost wheel and the summary execution of detail along the inside face of the wall.

30

Wooded Landscape with Wagon in a Glade

Early to mid 1760s
Black chalk and watercolour, heightened with white, 237 × 317 mm.
The Trustees of the British Museum, London
(1899-5-16-10, recto)
(Hayes, *Drawings*, no. 282)
[B]

31

Wooded Landscape with a Peasant asleep in a Cart

Early to mid 1760s
Watercolour and bodycolour, with traces of pencil, on brown paper, 281 × 380 mm.
The Visitors of the Ashmolean Museum, Oxford
(Hayes, *Drawings*, no. 266)

Both these sheets – of outstanding quality – are executed with the high degree of finish that characterises many of Gainsborough's drawings of the 1760s. Despite the differences in medium, the delicate, feathery quality of the foliage is comparable in both, and is similar to the handling of the trees in the Barber *Harvest Wagon*. As in the painting, Gainsborough's vantage-point is set low to impart a monumental quality to the landscape and figures, and to separate pictorial space from the viewer.

Here again, Gainsborough has employed his favoured strategy of angling a wagon on a path leading diagonally into a space screened with trees. As in the Barber picture, he has taken pains to inject a languid note into the setting, achieved in cat. 31 by the presence of a sleeping figure riding on the back of the cart (see also cat. 32), and in cat. 30, through the use of watercolour wash to suggest the deep shadows of a lazy summer afternoon. These are among the most accomplished of Gainsborough's drawings: more than mere studies or notations, they create a spirit of place and time that makes them works of art in their own right.

32

Wooded Landscape with Boy reclining in a Cart

Later 1760s
Pen and brown ink, with grey and brown washes, 181 × 237 mm.
The Trustees of the British Museum, London (1896-5-11-2)
(Hayes, *Drawings*, no. 307)
[T]

As a fully-worked drawing this sheet is unusual in that the cart motif has been brought close to the picture plane to dominate the composition. There is little doubt that it, and

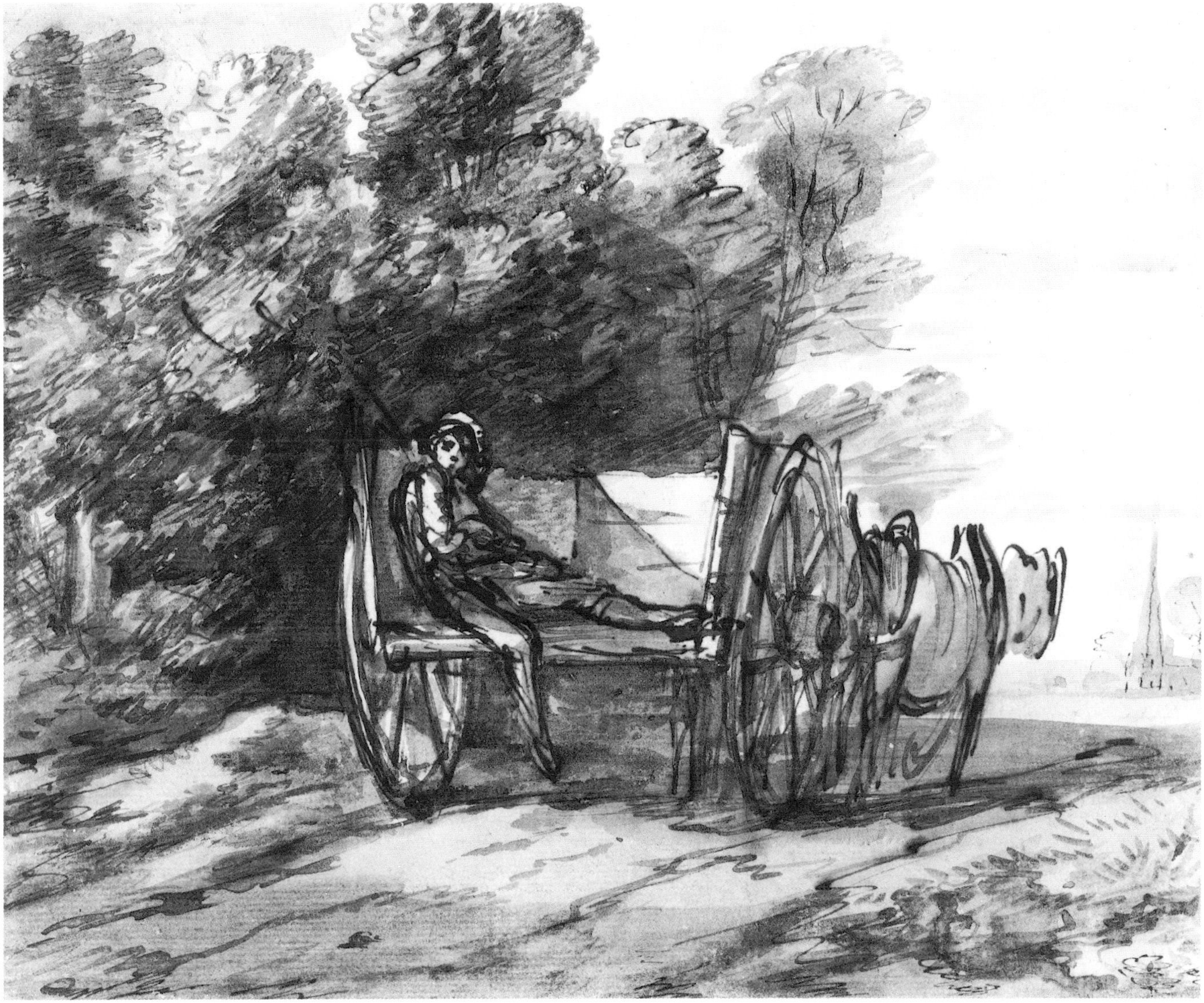

Cat. 32 Gainsborough, *Wooded Landscape with Boy reclining in a Cart*
The British Museum, London

not the landscape, is the subject here. The boy lounging idly in the back of the cart and staring at the viewer is equally untypical, and gives this delightful drawing the immediacy of reportage.

The dramatic chiaroscuro that bathes the undergrowth and cart in deep shadow and the bold outlines of the drawing are handled with the same remarkable fluency as Gainsborough's drawing of *A Woman seated with Three Children* (cat. 35).

33
Open Landscape with Figures in a Cart
Later 1770s
Black and white chalks on blue paper, 70 × 81 mm.
The Trustees of the British Museum, London (Oo.2-37)
(Hayes, *Drawings*, no. 417)

Hayes dates this tiny drawing to the late 1770s, thus between the execution of the Barber and Toronto *Harvest Wagons*. The wagon is here centered in the composition and pushed further into pictorial space, close to a large structure in the right background. The pyramidal group of figures from the Barber picture has survived (the heads aligned exactly along an imaginary diagonal from lower left to upper right), as has the animated lead horse (although here its head seems to be twisted back in the manner of Stubbs's *Horse Attacked by a Lion* pictures).

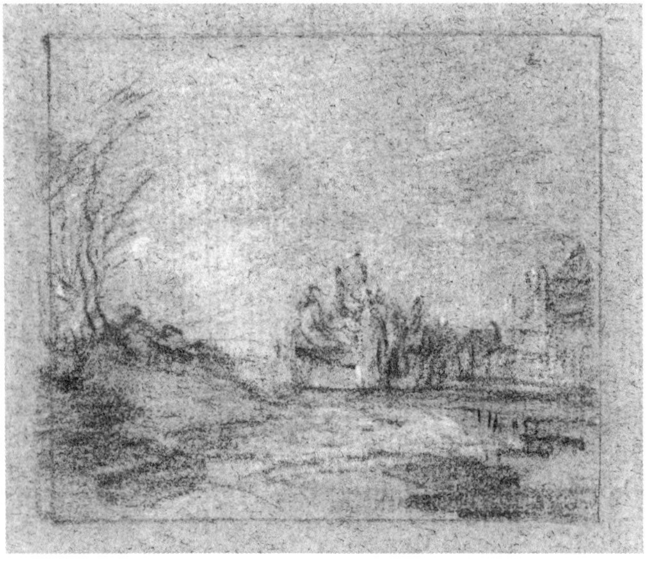

Cat. 33 Gainsborough, *Open Landscape with Figures in a Cart*
The British Museum, London

34
Wooded Landscape with Figure on Horseback and Packhorses
c. 1771–2
Black chalk, watercolour, bodycolour and lead white, 221 × 312 mm.
Inscribed in monogram, lower right: *TG*
Birmingham Museums and Art Gallery
(Hayes, *Drawings*, no. 333)

In this watercolour, Gainsborough has used reddish-brown paper dipped in skimmed milk and varnished to give an appearance of oil-finish.[1] The group of travellers is orientated in the same direction as those in *The Harvest Wagon*, and the use of highlights and streaks of light is comparable, particularly with the Barber version. Motifs such as the fallen tree and distant building are also common to both images, showing Gainsborough's inclination towards constant experiment and variation in his compositions. The foliage on the left has a shimmering quality which is achieved by the free use of small dabs of lead white, and may be compared with the thin but energetic handling of much of the foliage in the Barber *Harvest Wagon*. Gainsborough's stamped initials indicate his satisfaction with this watercolour, which he may have used as a presentation drawing. Many of his Bath period watercolours were highly finished with this in mind.

1 On this technique see further Jonathan P. Derow, 'Gainsborough's Varnished Watercolour Technique,' *Master Drawings*, XXVI, no. 3, Autumn 1988, pp. 259–271.

35

A Woman seated with Three Children

Black chalk and stump with red chalk on buff paper, heightened with white, 394 × 298 mm.

Inscribed lower left: *T. Gainsborough;* lower right: *Sketch given by D–*

The Trustees of the British Museum, London (1901-1-4-1)

(Hayes, *Drawings*, no. 839)

The composition of this undated drawing, with its spiralled, closely massed grouping of a woman, children and an infant against an architectural backdrop, first appears in *The Woodcutter's Return* of c. 1772–3,[1] and subsequently in the cottage door pictures that Gainsborough painted from c. 1778. Its thematic relationship to conventional allegorical representations of Charity has been noted.[2] More generically, this image of maternal devotion, fecundity and familial bliss is repeated in the figural group of the Toronto *Harvest Wagon*, where two young mothers are seated casually with their children, in poses that recall the traditional Madonna of Humility.

Gainsborough has taken pains to modulate broad areas of light and shadow in this drawing, and the dramatic chiaroscuro thus obtained is employed to similar effect in the Toronto painting.

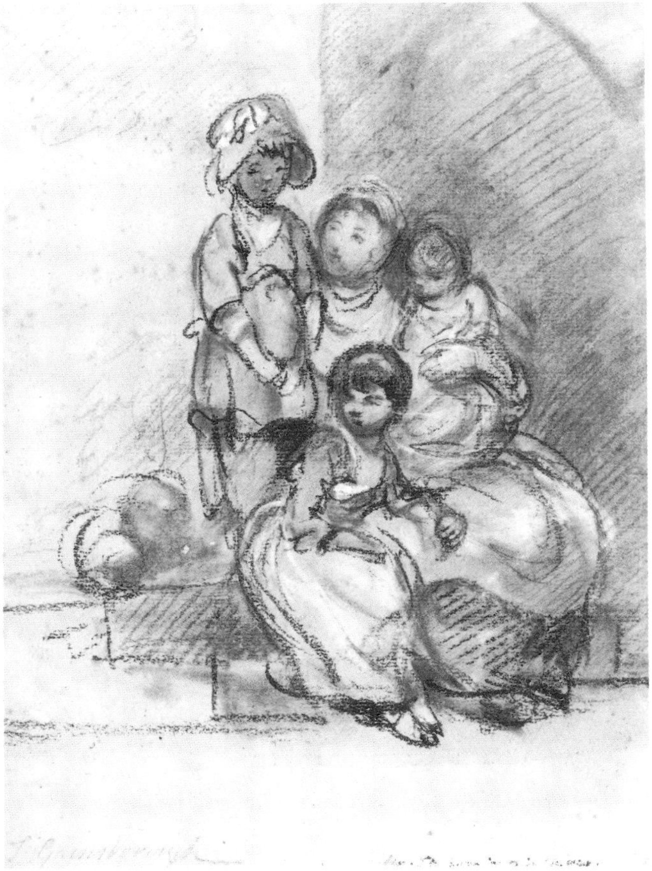

Cat. 35 Gainsborough, *A Woman seated with Three Children*
The British Museum, London

1 Hayes, no. 105.
2 London, British Museum, *Gainsborough and Reynolds in the British Museum*, cat. T. Clifford, A. Griffiths and M. Royalton-Kisch, 1978, no. 70.

36

Wooded Landscape with Country Cart

Black chalk and stump and white chalk on buff paper, 308 × 380 mm.

The Board of Trustees of the Victoria and Albert Museum, London (Dyce 671)

(Hayes, *Drawings*, no. 661)

This large and animated composition – all undulating lines, shadows and spotlighting – is dated by Hayes to the mid-1780s, and therefore to the period Gainsborough painted his second *Harvest Wagon*. While the theme and compositional details of the drawing are related only generically to the painting, both works reveal the artist's deep understanding and assimilation of Rubens's pictorial strategies during the last years of his life.

The siting of the cart on the path, the figure of the boy standing in the cart and the dog running from the left all appeared in Gainsborough's earlier soft ground etching, *Wooded Landscape with Two Country Carts and Figures* of 1779–1780 (cat. 38), where the vehicle is two, rather than four-wheeled.

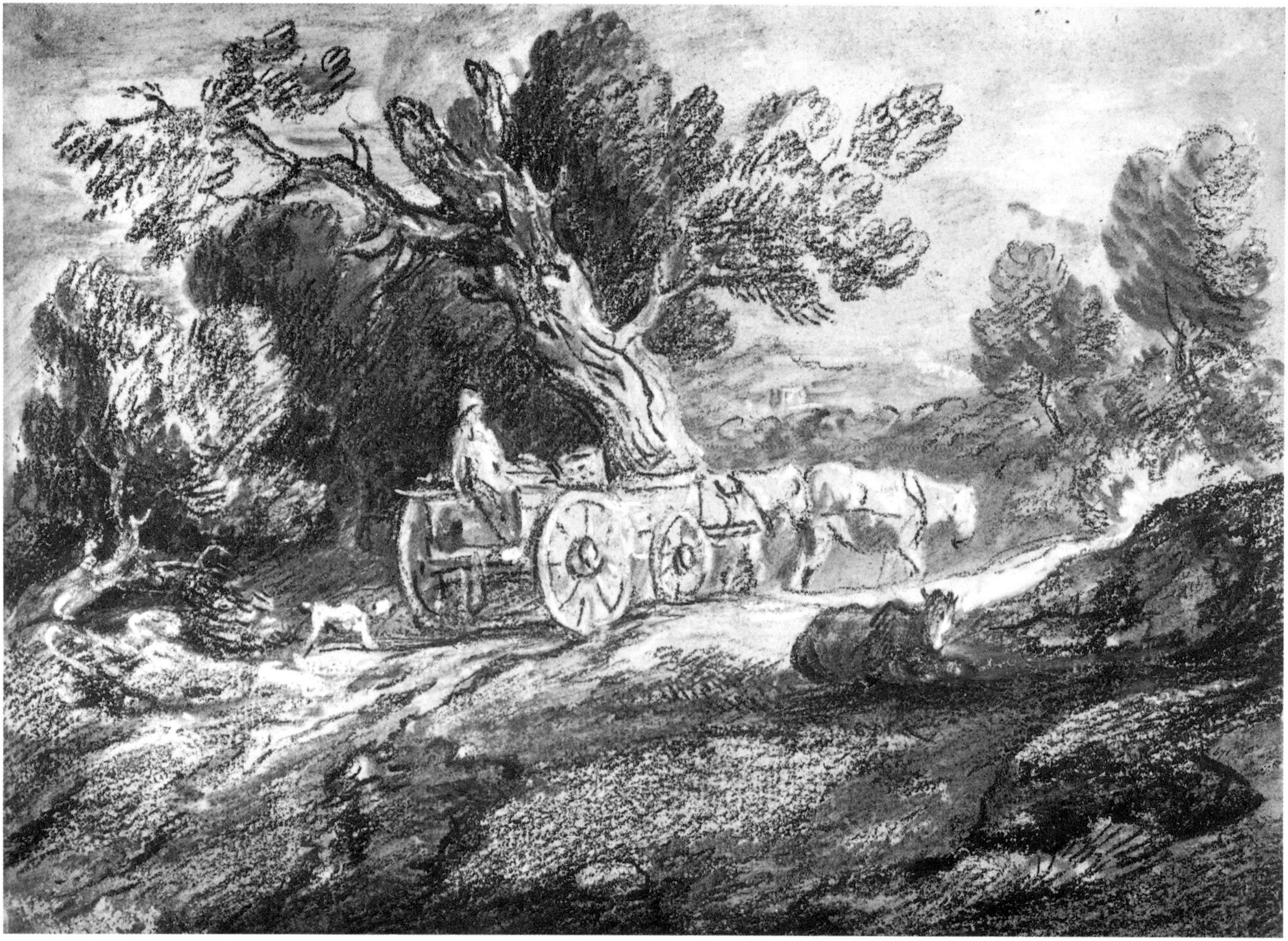

Cat. 36 Gainsborough, *Wooded Landscape with Country Cart*
The Victoria and Albert Museum, London

37

Wooded Landscape with Country Cart and Figures

c. 1774-1779

Soft ground etching with aquatint, 251 × 324 mm.

The Trustees of the British Museum, London

(1852-7-5-288)

(Hayes, *Gainsborough as Printmaker*, no. 6)

38

Wooded Landscape with Two Country Carts and Figures

1779–1780

Soft ground etching, 297 × 394 mm.

Inscribed on back of original mount: *Gainsborough fecit etch'd on a soft ground by him*

The Trustees of the British Museum, London

(1866-12-8-355)

(Hayes, *Gainsborough as Printmaker*, no. 9)

In the Barber and Toronto *Harvest Wagons*, and in several other paintings and drawings (see cats. 23 and 31), Gainsborough employed the device of the cart pulling away from the picture plane to lead the eye into the picture's space and to effect the transition between foreground and middle distance. In these two etchings the motif is used to the same end. In both, the massing of the composition is also similar to the *Harvest Wagons*, with the carts moving from left to right against a dark screen of foliage, along a track winding into the far central distance. Several additional analogies are worth noting. In cat. 37, the horse is posed in the same way as the first horse in the Toronto picture; the horse's drooping head and raised left leg in cat. 38 are repeated from the Barber canvas, and the little dog running below the cart reappears in the Toronto picture. The sharp angle between the two vehicles is close to that of the San Francisco *Wooded Landscape* which traditionally has been dated to c. 1778, about the date of this engraving (cat. 23). A later drawing (cat. 36) repeats several of the motifs, most notably the standing boy and the dog.

Gainsborough experimented only occasionally with the etching process, and had known the engraver and publisher, John Boydell, since 1747.[1] A drawing for cat. 37 at the Whitworth Art Gallery, University of Manchester,[2] corresponds to the etching in both composition and technique. Cat. 38 was pulled by the artist; both etchings were published by J. & J. Boydell in a series of twelve prints on 1 August 1797 (see cat. 39)

1 Hayes, pp. 37–39.
2 Hayes, *Drawings*, no. 407.
3 John Hayes, *Gainsborough as Printmaker* (New Haven and London, 1972), pp. 24–27.

39

Wooded Landscape with Country Cart and Figures

Soft ground etching, 251 × 322 mm.

Birmingham Museums and Art Gallery

(Hayes, *Gainsborough as Printmaker*, no. 12)

A late reprise, executed about 1783–6, of the motif of loaded country cart, seen from behind, proceeding through a winding, tree-lined lane. The prominent faggot-gatherer was a favourite motif of the artist in the 1780s (cf. *The Market Cart*, cat. 24). Gainsborough treated similar themes in his prints on several earlier occasions (cats. 37 and 38). Unlike these, however, the present example lacks the added tonality of aquatint. Of the twenty-two original prints by Gainsborough recorded, most date from the 1770s and 1780s and almost all are in soft ground etching, aquatint, or a combination of these media. They include some of his most brilliant and inventive productions. In 1797, John Boydell published the present example as the fifth in his series, *Twelve Prints of Landscape Scenery, with Cattle and figures [which] have never been worked up by another artist.*

The etching was known to Gainsborough's nephew and assistant, Gainsborough Dupont, who executed a related painting, formerly believed to be by Gainsborough himself.[1] This is in reverse orientation to the etching, but Dupont would have known the copper plate (now in the Tate Gallery, London) and may well have known an original drawing. His painting includes agitated clouds and fluent foliage, whereas the print seems empty and is predominantly linear – probably because Gainsborough's intention had been to add aquatint.

1 Birmingham Museum and Art Gallery, P.27'53; Hayes, p. 194, no. 14.

40
Edward Finden (1791–1857)
The Harvest Waggon (after Gainsborough)
1843
Line engraving, 355 × 503 mm.
Trustees of Gainsborough's House Society, Sudbury, Suffolk.

41
Richard Josey (1840 or 1841–1906)
The Hay Waggon (after Gainsborough)
Mezzotint, 137 × 163 mm.
Plate no. 117 of *Engravings from the Works of Thomas Gainsborough by J. Scott, G.H. Every, G. Sanders and other eminent Engravers*, Henry Graves & Co., London, n.d. [c.1880]
Trustees of Gainsborough's House Society, Sudbury, Suffolk.

Both these prints were published in the nineteenth century, at a time when the popularity of Gainsborough's landscapes was increasing in line with the general enthusiasm in Britain for landscape as a genre. Finden's *Harvest Waggon* (cat. 40) formed part of his *Royal Gallery of British Art*, published jointly with his brother, William. This came out in parts between 1838 and 1846, each print accompanied by a commentary. The present engraving is a faithful reproduction of the Barber *Harvest Waggon*. Indeed, it is more specific than the painting in its present state, clearly showing a church in the right background. It is noticeable, however, that the peasant controlling the leading horse has been domesticated in accordance with Victorian taste.

The title of Josey's *Hay Waggon* (cat. 41) reflects confusion as to the subject matter. Whether this is intended as an incident during haymaking or harvesting is far from explicit in the Barber *Harvest Waggon* itself, although the stalks in the wagon seem most likely to be wheat or barley. Josey's title may acknowledge the renown of Constable's *Hay Wain* (National Gallery, London), which, while remaining in private hands until 1886, was well known to the public through appearances at the International Exhibition, South Kensington, in 1862 and at the Royal Academy and the Burlington Fine Arts Club in 1871. Such a connection would be entirely appropriate in view of Constable's great admiration for Gainsborough.

42
Model of a Horse
Plaster, 17.8 × 24.8 × 7.6 cm.
Private Collection, United Kingdom
[B]

The pose and disposition of this model are very similar to the nearest horse in the Barber *Harvest Wagon*. Comparable weary-looking animals appear in *Peasant with Two Horses* (fig. 2) and many later landscapes by Gainsborough, who was attracted by their picturesque appearance. This was also recognised by his friend, Uvedale Price, who, in discussing "those animals that are called picturesque" identified "... among horses [...] the wild forester with his rough coat, his mane and tail ragged and uneven, or the worn-out cart-horse with his staring bones".[1]

Gainsborough is known to have made frequent use of models and objects when composing his landscapes, as was noted by his friend, William Jackson, who wrote of "little laymen for human figures and model horses and cows".[2] Reynolds described how "from the fields he brought into his painting room, stumps of trees, weeds, and animals of various kinds; and designed them, not from memory, but immediately from the objects. He even framed a kind of model of landskips, on his table; composed of broken stones, dried herbs, and pieces of looking-glass, which he magnified and improved into rocks, trees and water".[3] Later, W.H. Pyne commented on his use of cork, coal and broccoli as models while working at Bath.[4]

Model of a Horse, which was later acquired by John Constable, is the only surviving one of its kind, although several were extant in the decades following Gainsborough's death, including one which belonged to another painter, George Morland.[5]

1 An *Essay on the Picturesque*, 1796, p. 71.
2 William Jackson, *The Four Ages*, 1798, pp. 167–8. See also Mary Woodall, 'Gainsborough's Use of Models', *Antiques*, October 1956, pp. 363–5.
3 Sir Joshua Reynolds, *Discourses on Art*, ed. R. Wark, San Marino, 1959, Discourse XIV, p. 250.
4 *Somerset House Gazette*, 1824, quoted in Hayes, p. 33.
5 W. T. Whitley, *Art in England 1821–1837*, London,1930, p. 115.

Chronology

1727 Thomas Gainsborough born in Sudbury, Suffolk, the son of John Gainsborough, a successful cloth merchant, and his wife, Mary Burrough. He was baptised on 14 May, but his date of birth is unrecorded.

1740 Left Sudbury to study in London. Soon afterwards became a pupil of Hubert François Gravelot, French engraver and book illustrator, and began association with Francis Hayman.

c. 1745 Established himself as an independent artist in London.

1746 Married Margaret Burr, probably the illegitimate daughter of Frederick, Prince of Wales, at Dr Keith's Chapel, Mayfair.

1748 Returned with his wife to Sudbury after the death of his father.

1750 Birth of his elder surviving daughter, Mary.

1751 Birth of his younger daughter, Margaret.

1752 Moved to Ipswich.

1755 First London commission: two overmantel landscapes for the Duke of Bedford (see fig. 2).

1759 October: moved to Bath.

1761 First exhibited at the Society of Artists, Spring Gardens, London.

1767 Exhibited the Barber *Harvest Wagon* (cat. 1) at the Society of Artists.

1768 Invited to become a founder-member of the Royal Academy, the only artist working outside London to be so.

1769 Exhibited at the first Royal Academy exhibition, where his *Portrait of Lady Molyneux* (Walker Art Gallery, Liverpool) was a resounding success.

1771 May have exhibited the Barber *Harvest Wagon* at the Royal Academy, together with *Rocky Wooded Landscape with Rustic Lovers* (cat. 14).

1772 Took his nephew, Gainsborough Dupont, as his apprentice. Dupont was his only recorded pupil.

1773 Refused to exhibit at the Royal Academy again (until 1777) owing to a quarrel about the hanging of his pictures.

1774 Presented the Barber *Harvest Wagon* to Walter Wiltshire on leaving Bath for London. Took a lease on the west wing of Schomberg House, Pall Mall.

1777 Received his first commission from the Royal Family: full length portraits of the Duke and Duchess of Cumberland.

1780 Exhibited six landscapes which were said to "beggar description" at the Royal Academy, in addition to major portraits.

1781 Exhibited full-length portraits of George III and Queen Charlotte at the Royal Academy, after which he received numerous royal commissions.

c. 1782 Went on a tour of the West Country with Gainsborough Dupont.

1783 Went on a tour of the Lake District with Samuel Kilderbee.

c. 1783 Constructed a peep-show box in which he displayed glass transparencies (now in the Victoria and Albert Museum, London).

1784 Began the Toronto *Harvest Wagon*. (cat. 2). Ceased exhibiting at the Royal Academy and mounted a series of annual exhibitions in his studio at Schomberg House.

1788 Died 2 August and was buried in Kew Churchyard, London.

1789 Private sale of his pictures and drawings held at Schomberg House, at which the Toronto *Harvest Wagon* was included as from the Prince of Wales's collection. (Additional sales were held at Christie's in 1792; 1797 following the death of Gainsborough Dupont; and 1799, following the death of Mrs Gainsborough).

The Barber *Harvest Wagon*

PROVENANCE

Given by Gainsborough in 1774 to Walter Wiltshire (c. 1719–1799) of Shockerwick Park, near Bath;
His son, John Wiltshire;
John Wiltshire sale; Christie's, London, 25 May 1867, lot 126, bought Davis, 2,950 guineas;
Sir Dudley Majoribanks, later Lord Tweedmouth (1820–1894);
Sold privately to Sir Samuel Montagu, later Lord Swaythling (1832–1911), Townhill Park, Southampton;
Swaythling sale, Christie's, 12 July 1946, lot 20; bought Barber Institute.

EXHIBITIONS

London, Society of Artists, 1767, no. 61
London, British Institution, *Pictures by the Late William Hogarth, Richard Wilson, Thomas Gainsborough and J. Zoffany*, 1814, no. 37
London, Royal Academy, *Old Masters*, 1880, no. 140
London, Grosvenor Gallery, *Works of Thomas Gainsborough*, 1885, no. 33
London, Royal Academy, *Old Masters*, 1896. no. 94
Paris, Exposition Universelle, British Pavilion, 1900, no. 63
London, Royal Academy, *Old Masters*, 1907, no. 109
Berlin, Königliche Akademie der Künste, *Old English Masters*, 1908, no. 64
Copenhagen, Ny Carlsberg Glyptotek, *Aeldre Engelsk Künst*, 1908, no. 7
Wembley, British Empire Exhibition, Palace of Arts, 1924, no. V. 28.
Ipswich, *Bicentenary Exhibition of Thomas Gainsborough R.A.*, 1927, no. 55
Vienna, Sezession, *Meisterwerke Englische Malerei aus Dreijahrhunderten*, 1927, no. 24
Brussels, Musée Moderne, *Exposition Rétrospective de Peinture Anglaise (XVIIIe et XIXe Siècles)*, 1929, no. 64
London, Royal Academy, *Exhibition of British Art c. 1000–1860*, 1934, no. 332 (Commemorative Catalogue no. 192).
Brussels, *Exposition Universelle et Internationale*, 1935, no. 1109
London, 45, Park Lane, *Gainsborough Loan Exhibition*, 1936, no. 100
Winchester College, *Old Masters from Hampshire Houses*, 1938, no. 21
Paris, Louvre, *La Peinture Anglaise XVIIIe et XIXe Siècles*, 1938, no. 49
London, Arts Council, *Thomas Gainsborough*, 1953, no. 32
Munich, Residenz, *Europaïsches Rokoko*, 1958, no. 65
London, Royal Academy, *Bicentenary Exhibition 1768–1968*, 1968–9, no. 142
London, Tate Gallery, *Landscape in Britain, c. 1750–c. 1850*, 1973–4, no. 57
Paris, Grand Palais, *Gainsborough 1727–1788*, 1981, no. 42
Bath, Holburne Museum and Craft Study Centre, *Gainsborough in Bath*, 1988, no. 34

BIBLIOGRAPHY

Anon., *A Critical Examination of the Pictures*, London, 1767, p. 9
Allan Cunningham, *The Lives of the Most Eminent British Painters, Sculptors and Architects*, London, I, 1829, pp. 330-1
Edward and William Finden, *The Royal Gallery of British Art*, n.d. [1843], unpaginated, engr. facing text
George Williams Fulcher, *Life of Thomas Gainsborough, R.A.*, London, 1856, pp. 70–71, 199
John Timbs, *Anecdote Biography*, London, 1860, p. 162
J. Beavington-Atkinson, 'Thomas Gainsborough'. Article in Robert Dohme, *Kunst und Künstler des Mittelalters und der Neuzeit*, Leipzig, VI, 1880
Engravings from the Works of Thomas Gainsborough, R.A., Henry Graves and Company, London, n.d. [c. 1880], no. 117
George M. Brock-Arnold, *Gainsborough*, London, 1881, p. 34
William Martin Conway, *The Artistic Development of Reynolds and Gainsborough*, London, 1886, pp. 54, 82–3
Sir Walter Armstrong, *Thomas Gainsborough*, London, 1894, pp. 32, 60, 82
Mrs Arthur Bell, *Thomas Gainsborough: A Record of his Life and Works*, London, 1897, pp. 66–7, 122, repr. facing p. 64
Sir Walter Armstrong, *Gainsborough & his Place in English Art*, London, 1898, pp. 114, 118, 208
Georges Lafenestre, 'La peinture ancienne a l'Exposition Universelle,' *Gazette des Beaux-Arts*, XXIV, December 1900, p. 560
Mrs Arthur Bell, *Thomas Gainsborough, R.A.*, London, 1902, pp. 9, 55
Lord Ronald Sutherland Gower, *Thomas Gainsborough*, London, 1903, pp. 52, 113, 127, repr. facing p. 58
Arthur B. Chamberlain, *Thomas Gainsborough*, London, n.d. [1903], pp. 78, 158
Sir Walter Armstrong, *Gainsborough & his Place in English Art*, London, 1904, pp. 151, 156, 157, 283
A. E. Fletcher, *Thomas Gainsborough, R.A.*, New York, 1904, pp. 82, 88, 93, 98
William B. Boulton, *Thomas Gainsborough, His Life, Works, Friends and Sitters*, London, 1905, pp. 95, 141–2, 153
Sir Walter Armstrong, *Thomas Gainsborough*, 1906, pp. 82, 204
Algernon Graves, *The Society of Artists of Great Britain, 1760–1791*, London, 1907, p. 98

Mortimer Menpes and James Greig, *Gainsborough*, London, 1909, pp. 80, 90, 95, 174
Myra Reynolds, *The Treatment of Nature in English Poetry*, Chicago, 1909, p. 306
Art Journal, March 1911, repr. p. 96
William T. Whitley, *Thomas Gainsborough*, London, 1915, pp. 40, 50-51
E. Rimbault Dibdin, *Thomas Gainsborough*, London, 1923, p. 85
R. H. Wilenski, 'The Gainsborough Bicentenary Exhibition,' *Apollo*, VI, November 1927, p. 195
Frank Rutter, 'The Gainsborough Bicentenary Exhibition,' *Sunday Times*, 9 October 1927, p. 13
William T. Whitley, *Artists and their Friends in England 1700–1799*, London and Boston, 1928, II, p. 65
Charles Johnson, *English Painting from the Seventh Century to the Present Day*, London, 1932, pp. 130, 133, 134, repr. facing p. 134
C. H. Collins Baker, *British Painting*, London, 1933, p. 151
R. H. Wilenski, *English Painting*, London, 1933, pp. 115–6
Herbert Read, 'English Art,' *Burlington Magazine*, LXIII, December 1933, repr. pl. VIIIB
Charles Johnson, *A Short Account of British Painting*, London, 1934, p. 55
London, Royal Academy, *Commemorative Catalogue of the Exhibition of British Art*, 1935, no. 192, repr. pl. LXIII
Ellis K. Waterhouse, 'Gainsborough in Park Lane: Exhibition at Sir Philip Sassoon's,' *Connoisseur*, XCVII, March 1936, p. 124
Mary Woodall, *Gainsborough's Landscape Drawings*, London, 1939, pp. 17, 20, 44–8, 49, 54–5, 56, 57, 61, 72, 110, repr. pl. 40
Oliver Millar, *Thomas Gainsborough*, London, 1949, pp. 9–10, repr. pl. 25
Mary Woodall, *Thomas Gainsborough: His Life and Work*, London, 1949, pp. 68, 91–3, 95, repr. facing p. 80 (col.)
Mary Woodall, 'The Gainsborough Exhibition at Bath,' *Burlington Magazine*, XCIII, August 1951, p. 266
Ellis K. Waterhouse, 'The Exhibition "The First Hundred Years of the Royal Academy",' *Burlington Magazine*, XCIV, February 1952, p. 51
Catalogue of the Paintings, Drawings and Miniatures in the Barber Institute of Fine Arts, Cambridge, 1952, pp. 38–9, repr. p. 41
Ernest Short, *A History of British Painting*, London, 1953, p. 172
Ellis K. Waterhouse, *Painting in Britain 1530–1790*, Harmondsworth, 1953, pp. 188–9, 231, repr. pl. 154
David Piper, 'Gainsborough at the Tate Gallery,' *Burlington Magazine*, XCV, July 1953, p. 246
C. H. Collins Baker, 'The Kennedy Memorial Gallery,' CXXXIV, *Connoisseur*, October 1954, p. 140
Ellis K. Waterhouse, *Gainsborough*, London, 1958, pp. 24, 34, 40, no. 907, repr. pl. 99
Mary Woodall, 'Gainsborough Landscapes at Nottingham University,' *Burlington Magazine*, CIV, December 1962, p. 562
Mary Woodall, *The Letters of Thomas Gainsborough*, London, 1963, repr. facing p. 112 (detail)
John Hayes, 'Gainsborough and Rubens,' *Apollo*, LXXVIII, August 1963, pp. 92, 94, repr. fig. 5 (detail)
Jonathan Norton Leonard *et al.*, *The World of Gainsborough, 1727–1788*, New York, 1969, pp. 65, 180–3
John Hayes, *The Drawings of Thomas Gainsborough*, London and New Haven, 2 vols., 1970, pp. 38, 175, 205, 297, 300, repr. pl. 330
Mary Webster, *Francis Wheatley*, London, 1970, pp. 14, 118, repr. fig. 11
William Gaunt, *The Great Century of British Painting: Hogarth to Turner*, London, 1971, repr. pl. 56
Jean-Jacques Mayoux, *La peinture anglaise de Hogarth aux Préraphaélites*, Geneva, 1972, pp. 71–2, repr. p. 72 (col.)
Norman Johnsen, *A Study of the Mature Oil Painting Styles and Techniques of Thomas Gainsborough*, unpublished M.A. thesis, University of Birmingham, 1972, pp. 7, 10, 22–3, 49, 83, 84, 87, 100, 101
Luke Herrmann, *British Landscape Painting of the Eighteenth Century*, London, 1973, pp. 96–7, 103, 104, 117, repr. pl. XII (col.)
John Hayes, *Gainsborough: Paintings and Drawings*, London, 1975, pp. 43 and 213, no. 61; repr. pls 77, 80 (detail)
Ronald Paulson, *Emblem and Expression: Meaning in English Art of the Eighteenth Century*, London, 1975, p. 247
Isabelle Worman, *Thomas Gainsborough: A Biography 1727–1788*, Lavenham, 1976, pp. 63–4, 83, 85, 122
David Coombs, *Sport and the Countryside*, Oxford, 1978, p. 49, repr.
Marcia Pointon, 'Gainsborough and the Landscape of Retirement,' *Art History*, II-4, December 1979, p. 453
John Barrell, *The Dark Side of the Landscape: The Rural Poor in English Painting, 1730–1840*, Cambridge, 1980, pp. 59–62, 64, 69, 70, 109, repr. pp. 59, 60 (detail)
John Hayes, *Thomas Gainsborough*, exh. cat., London, Tate Gallery, 1980, p. 27
Dillian Gordon, *Second Sight: Rubens: The Watering Place/Gainsborough: The Watering Place*, exh. cat., London, National Gallery, 1981, p. 18, repr. fig. 21
Jack Lindsay, *Thomas Gainsborough: His Life and Art*, London, 1981, pp. 79, 86, 120, 187
Ellis K. Waterhouse, *The Dictionary of British 18th Century Painters*, Woodbridge, 1981, p. 138
Christopher White, 'Rubens and British Art, 1630–1790,' in *"Sind Briten hier?": Relations between British and Continental Art, 1680–1880*, Munich, 1981, pp. 39–42, repr.
Michael Rosenthal, *English Landscape Painting*, Oxford, 1982, pp. 58, 68, 82–6, repr. pl. 62
John Hayes, *The Landscape Paintings of Thomas Gainsborough: A Critical Text and Catalogue Raisonné*, London and Ithaca, 1982, I, pp. 24, 102–4, 107, 110, 120, 123, (nn. 59, 63), 124 (n. 96), 145, 151, 158 (n. 86), 237, 238, 280, 291, 313, 325, pls. 133, 137, 217; II, no. 88 and under nos. 89, 113, 119, 157

Hamish Miles and Paul Spencer-Longhurst, *Handbook of the Barber Institute of Fine Arts*, Birmingham, 1983, p. 14
Ann Sumner, 'Springs of Inspiration,' *Country Life*, CLXXXII, 7 July 1988, p. 152
Malcolm Cormack, *The Paintings of Thomas Gainsborough*, Cambridge, 1991, pp. 88–9
Ian G. Lumsden, *Gainsborough in Canada*, exh. cat., Fredericton (NB), Beaverbrook Art Gallery, 1991, pp. 48–9, under no. 12
Stephen Butler, *Gainsborough*, London, 1992, p. 88
Paul Spencer-Longhurst, *The Barber Institute of Fine Arts Handbook*, Birmingham, 1993, p. 42
Michael Rosenthal in *Glorious Nature: British Landscape Painting 1750–1850*, exh. cat. Denver Art Museum, 1993, by Katherine Baetjer and others, pp. 22–3
Gainsborough and Reynolds: Contrasts in Royal Patronage, exh. cat., London, The Queen's Gallery, Buckingham Palace, 1994, p. 11

The Toronto *Harvest Wagon*

PROVENANCE

George, Prince of Wales (George IV, King of Great Britain and Ireland from 1820) (acquired from the artist by 1786 and paid for in 1793);
Mrs. Maria Fitzherbert (gift from the Prince of Wales, 1810–1837);
George Damer (by descent, 1837; sold, London, Christie's, [Col. George-Lionel Dawson Damer] sale, 27 March 1841, lot 141, 620 guineas);
John Gibbons, Birmingham;
The Rev. Benjamin Gibbons (by descent, 1851–1894; sold London, Christie's, Gibbons sale, 26 May 1894, lot 24, 4500 guineas);
Colnaghi, London;
Lionel (later Sir Lionel) Phillips (1898–1913; sold London, Christie's, Phillips sale, 25 April 1913, lot 45, 19,200 guineas to Lockett Agnew for Judge Elbert H. Gary);
Judge Elbert H. Gary, New York, (1913–1928; sold New York, Gary Sale, American Art Association, 20 April 1928, lot 30, $360,000 to Duveen);
Mr. and Mrs. Frank P. Wood, Toronto (1928?–1941); Gift to Art Gallery of Ontario.

EXHIBITIONS

London, Schomberg House, 30 March–31 May 1789, no. 74 (as "A Landscape, with a Waggon and Figures returning from Market," described with the next picture as "his Royal Highness the Prince of Wales's, ...not yet sent Home")
London, British Institution, *Pictures by the Late William Hogarth, Richard Wilson, Thomas Gainsborough and J. Zoffany*, 1814, no. 13
London, British Institution, *The Works of Ancient Masters and Deceased British Artists*, 1841, no. 127
London, Royal Academy, 1870, no. 82
London, Royal Academy, *Works by the Old Masters and by Deceased Masters of the British School*, Winter 1890, no. 163
London, Agnew's, *20 Masterpieces of the English School*, 1895, no. 5
London, The New Gallery, *Pictures by Masters of the Flemish and British Schools*, 1899–1900, no. 181
Toronto, Art Gallery of Toronto, *A Loan Collection of Paintings by Old Masters . . .*, 1929, no. 5
New York World's Fair, *European Paintings and Sculpture from 1300–1800: Masterpieces of Art*, 1939, no. 131
New York, Knoedler Galleries, *Loan Exhibition of Allied Art for Allied Aid*, 1940, no. 7
Montreal, Art Association of Montreal, *Loan Exhibition of Masterpieces of Painting*, 1942, no. 88
Toronto, Art Gallery of Toronto, *Loan Exhibition of Great Paintings in Aid of Allied Merchant Seamen*, 1944, no. 21
Providence (RI), Rhode Island School of Design, Museum of Art, *Old and New England*, 1945, no. 71
Boston, Museum of Fine Arts, *A Thousand Years of Landscape East and West*, 1945, p. 7
St. Louis, City Art Museum, *40 Masterpieces: A Loan Exhibition of Paintings from American Museums*, 1947, no. 16
Montreal, Montreal Museum of Fine Arts, *The Eighteenth Century: Art of France and England*. 1950, no. 4
Toronto, Art Gallery of Toronto; Montreal, Montreal Museum of Fine Arts; Ottawa, National Gallery of Canada, *Paintings by European Masters from Public and Private Collections in Toronto, Montreal and Ottawa*, 1954, no. 34
Detroit, Detroit Institute of Arts; Philadelphia, Philadelphia Museum of Art, *Romantic Art in Britain: Paintings and Drawings 1760–1860*, 1968, no. 22
Baltimore, Baltimore Museum of Art, *From El Greco to Pollock: Early and Late Works by European and American Artists*, 1968, no. 26
Providence (RI), Brown University, Bell Gallery, *Rubenism*, 1975, no. 67 and pp. 200, 202
London, Tate Gallery, *Thomas Gainsborough*, 1980–81, no. 150
Paris, Grand Palais, *Gainsborough 1727–1788*, 1981, no. 73
Fredericton (NB), Beaverbrook Art Gallery, *Gainsborough in Canada*, 1991, no. 12

BIBLIOGRAPHY

Henry Bate-Dudley. In: *Morning Herald*, 27 January 1785, p. 2

Henry Bate-Dudley. In: *Morning Herald*, 3 April 1786, p. 2

Morning Post, 30 March 1789, p. 3

Morning Herald, 11 June 1789

George Williams Fulcher, *Life of Thomas Gainsborough, R.A.*, London, 1856, pp. 193, 233

[J. S.], *Notes and Queries*, 25 November 1871, p. 434

Sir Walter Armstrong, *Thomas Gainsborough*, London, 1894, p. 50

Mrs. Arthur Bell, *Thomas Gainsborough: A Record of his Life and Works*, London, 1897, pp. 122–123

Sir Walter Armstrong, *Gainsborough & his Place in English Art*, London, 1898, pp. 114, 117–118, 207, repr. facing p. 40

Lord Ronald Sutherland Gower, *Thomas Gainsborough*, London, 1903, p. 113, repr. facing p. 52

Sir Walter Armstrong, *Gainsborough & his Place in English Art*, London, 1904, pp. 151, 156–157, 283

Sir Walter Armstrong, *Thomas Gainsborough*, London, 1906, pp. 131, 157

Mortimer Menpes and James Greig, *Gainsborough*, London, 1909, p. 80

William T. Whitley, *Thomas Gainsborough*, London, 1915, pp. 235, 258–259, 322, 332

William T. Whitley, *Artists and their Friends in England 1700–1799*, London & Boston, 1928, II, pp. 63–64, 66 and pl. 3

'Gainsborough Sets Record of $360,000 at Gary Art Sale,' *The New York Times*, 21 April 1928

'Gary Art Sale Sets Record at $2,297,763,' *The New York Times*, 21 April 1928

Esther Singleton, *Old World Masters in New World Collections*, New York, 1929, pp. 389–392 ill.

C. H. Collins Baker, *British Painting*, London, 1933, pp. 108, 151

Mary Woodall, *Gainsborough's Landscape Drawings*, Boston, 1939, pp. 81–82

T. Craven, *A Treasury of Art Masterpieces*, New York, 1939, p. 414 and pl. 100

William R. Valentiner, *Masterpieces of Art: Exhibition at the New York World's Fair 1939*, New York, 1939, pl. 113.

Shane Leslie, *Mrs. Fitzherbert; A Life Chiefly from Unpublished Sources*, New York, 1939, p. 386

'Toronto Acquires,' *Art News*, XLI (1–14 December 1942), p. 35

[Tancred Borenius], 'Gainsborough's Collection of Pictures,' *Burlington Magazine*, LXXIV, May 1944, p. 109

Ellis K. Waterhouse, 'A Gainsborough Bill for the Prince of Wales,' *Burlington Magazine*, LXXXVIII, November 1946, p. 276

Mary Woodall, *Thomas Gainsborough: His Life and Work*, London, 1949, p. 92n

'The Auction Picture,' *Art Digest*, 1 November 1951, p. 38

S. N. Behrman, *Duveen*, New York, 1951, p. 144

R. H. Hubbard, 'Art Museums in Canada: Some Developments in 1953–4,' *Art Quarterly*, LXVII (Winter 1954), pp. 354, repr. 360

R. H. Hubbard, *European Paintings in Canadian Collections; Earlier Schools*, Toronto, 1956, pp. xxiv, 116 and pl. LV

Ellis K. Waterhouse, *Gainsborough*, London, 1958, pp. 19, 34, no. 993 repr. pl. 270

[Art Gallery of Ontario], *Painting and Sculpture*, Toronto, 1959, p. 28

John Hayes, 'Gainsborough and Rubens,' *Apollo*, LXXVIII, August 1963, pp. 94–95 and fig. 9

John Hayes, 'Gainsborough's Later Landscapes,' *Apollo*, LXXX, July 1964, p. 26

Ronald Freyberger, 'The Judge Elbert H. Gary Sale,' *Auction*, II-10, June 1969, p. 11

Oliver Millar, *The Later Georgian Pictures in the Collection of Her Majesty the Queen*, London, 1969, I, pp. xxvi, 35 and fig. XIX

Wesley Towner, *The Elegant Auctioneers*, New York, 1970, pp. 444–445

R.E. [Ralph Edwards], 'Review of Oliver Millar, *Later Georgian Pictures . . .' Connoisseur*, CLXXIV, July 1970, p. 212

Geoffrey Williamson, *The Ingeneous Mr. Gainsborough*, London, 1972, p. 188

Luke Herrmann, *British Landscape Painting of the Eighteenth Century*, London, 1973, p. 104

Gerald Reitlinger, 'Return of the Duveen Market?' *Art at Auction: The Year at Sotheby Parke Bernet 1972–73*, New York, 1974, p. 58, repr.

William J. Withrow, *Art Gallery of Ontario: Handbook/Catalogue illustré*, Toronto, 1974, pp. 2, 63, repr.

John Hayes, *Gainsborough: Paintings and Drawings*, London, 1975, pp. 44, 47, no. 114 and pl. 78

Ronald Paulson, *Emblem and Expression: Meaning in English Art of the Eighteenth Century*, London, 1975, p. 247, n. 40

Timothy Clifford, Antony Griffiths and Martin Royalton-Kisch, *Gainsborough and Reynolds in the British Museum*, exh. cat. London, British Museum, 1978, p. 22

John Barrell, *The Dark Side of the Landscape: The Rural Poor in English Painting 1730–1840*, Cambridge, 1980, pp. 68–70, 109 and pp. 67–68, repr.

John Ingamells, 'Review of *Thomas Gainsborough*,' *Burlington Magazine*, CXXII, November 1980, p. 780

Dillian Gordon, *Second Sight: Rubens: The Watering Place/ Gainsborough: The Watering Place*, exh. cat., London, National Gallery, 1981, p. 19

Jack Lindsay, *Thomas Gainsborough: His Life and Art*, London, 1981, pp. 64, 168 and pl. 8

Christoph Heilmann, 'Review of *Thomas Gainsborough*,' *Kunstchronik*, XXXIV, March 1981, p. 116

John Hayes, *The Landscape Paintings of Thomas Gainsborough: A Critical Text and Catalogue Raisonné*, London and Ithaca, 1982, I, pp. 145, 147, 182, 232 and pl. 180; II, no. 157 and pp. 316, 325

Jennifer C. Watson, 'Review of John Barrell, *The Dark Side of the Landscape*,' RACAR, X-2 (1983), p. 220, fig. 3

Thomas E. Norton, *100 Years of Collecting in America: The Story of Sotheby Parke Bernet*, New York, 1984, p. 106
F. J. P. B. [Francis Broun], *Gainsborough* (Masterpieces in the Collection of the Art Gallery of Ontario), Toronto, 1984
E. D. H. Johnson, *Paintings of the British Social Scene from Hogarth to Sickert*, New York, 1986, p. 118
Masterpieces from the Art Gallery of Ontario, Toronto, 1987, pp. 34–35 repr.
Art Gallery of Ontario: Selected Works, Toronto, 1990, p. 123
Paul Jeromack, 'Judge Gary, the Collector and his Gold Service,' In: New York, Sotheby's, 19 October 1994, n.p.

List of Lenders

The Hon. C. A. Lennox-Boyd 20
The Earl of Yarmouth, Ragley Hall 22, 27
Private Collections, United Kingdom 6, 8, 14, 16, 28, 29, 42

The Trustees of the Barber Institute of Fine Arts, The University of Birmingham 1, 10
Birmingham Museums and Art Gallery 34, 39
London, The Trustees of the British Museum 9, 17, 18, 30, 32, 33, 35, 37, 38
London, The Iveagh Bequest, Kenwood (English Heritage) 13
London, The Trustees of the National Gallery 24
London, The National Portrait Gallery 4
London, Tate Gallery 12
London, The Board of Trustees of the Victoria and Albert Museum 36
City of Nottingham Museums, Castle Museum and Art Gallery 15
Oxford, The Visitors of the Ashmolean Museum 5, 31
Rothschild Trust, Canada, Inc. 3
The Fine Arts Museums of San Francisco 21, 23
Southampton City Art Gallery 7
Sudbury, The Trustees of Gainsborough's House Society 40, 41
The Toledo Museum of Art 25
Toronto, Art Gallery of Ontario 2, 11, 26
Washington (DC), National Gallery of Art 19

Photographic Credits

Plate III	The Ashmolean Museum, Oxford.
Fig. 2	By kind permission of the Marquess of Tavistock and the Trustees of the Bedford Estate.
Fig. 4	The Barber Institute of Fine Arts, The University of Birmingham.
Fig. 6	Neue Pinakothek, Bayerische Staatsgemäldesammlungen, Munich.
Fig. 8	© 1979 Sotheby's Inc.
Cat. 3	Christies Images, London.
Cat. 16	Courtauld Institute of Art, London.
Cat. 24	Reproduced by courtesy of the Trustees, The National Gallery, London.